STUDY GUIDE TO ACCOMPANY

DONATED BY:

THE RESTAURANT
From Concept to Operation

FIFTH EDITION

JOHN R. WALKER, D.B.A., C.H.A., F.M.P.

SAN IGNACIO COLLEGE
LIBRARY

JOHN WILEY and SONS, INC.

This book is printed on acid-free paper. ∞

Copyright © 2008 by John Wiley and Sons, Inc. All rights reserved

Published by John Wiley and Sons, Inc., Hoboken, New Jersey.
Published simultaneously in Canada.

Wiley Bicentennial Logo Design by Richard J. Pacifico.

No part of this publication may be reproduced, stored in a retrieval system, or transmitted in any form or by any means, electronic, mechanical, photocopying, recording, scanning, or otherwise, except as permitted under Section 107 or 108 of the 1976 United States Copyright Act, without either the prior written permission of the Publisher, or authorization through payment of the appropriate per-copy fee to the Copyright Clearance Center, Inc., 222 Rosewood Drive, Danvers, MA 01923, 978-750-8400, fax 978-646-8600, or on the web at www.copyright.com. Requests to the Publisher for permission should be addressed to the Permissions Department, John Wiley and Sons, Inc., 111 River Street, Hoboken, NJ 07030, 201-748-6011, fax 201-748-6008, or online at http://www.wiley.com/go/permissions.

Limit of Liability/Disclaimer of Warranty: While the publisher and author have used their best efforts in preparing this book, they make no representations or warranties with respect to the accuracy or completeness of the contents of this book and specifically disclaim any implied warranties of merchantability or fitness for a particular purpose. No warranty may be created or extended by sales representatives or written sales materials. The advice and strategies contained herein may not be suitable for your situation. You should consult with a professional where appropriate. Neither the publisher nor author shall be liable for any loss of profit or any other commercial damages, including but not limited to special, incidental, consequential, or other damages.

For general information on our other products and services, or technical support, please contact our Customer Care Department within the United States at 800-762-2974, outside the United States at 317-572-3993 or fax 317-572-4002.

Wiley also publishes its books in a variety of electronic formats. Some content that appears in print may not be available in electronic books.

For more information about Wiley products, visit our Web site at http://*www.wiley.com*.

Library of Congress Cataloging-in-Publication Data:

ISBN 13: 978-0-470-14059-8

Printed in the United States of America

10   9   8   7   6   5   4   3   2   1

TABLE OF CONTENTS

To the Student

This Study Guide is a companion to *The Restaurant: From Concept to Operation*, Fifth Edition. It serves as a resource to help you study and review the material in the text. This supplement is arranged by chapter corresponding to the 16 chapters in *The Restaurant*. Holly E. Carvalho has helped to prepare the features within this supplement to ensure that each chapter includes several resources to help you review the material and exercises that you can use to test your own knowledge of the key topics and concepts. These resources include the following:

Objectives
These highlight the key concepts presented in the chapter and provide a road map of the specific knowledge and skills you should be learning from reading the chapter.

Chapter Outline
Provides a detailed summary of the key points presented in the chapter.

True or False
True or False questions are provided for each chapter. These questions test your understanding of key terms and concepts.

Fill in the Blank: Key Term Review
Key Term Review questions ask you to fill in the blanks with the appropriate term or phrase to complete the sentence and help to reinforce your comprehension of the concepts presented in the chapter.

Multiple Choice Questions: Concept Review
Multiple Choice Questions ask you to choose the most appropriate response to each question. These questions ensure that you fully comprehend the key concepts covered in each chapter.

Short Answer Questions
Thought-provoking questions based upon the material presented in the chapter test the knowledge you have gained from studying the chapter.

You can check your answers at the end of the Study Guide after completing the exercises in each chapter.

CHAPTER 1: INTRODUCTION

OBJECTIVES

- Discuss reasons why some people open restaurants.

- List some challenges of restaurant operation.

- Outline the history of restaurants.

- Compare the advantages and disadvantages of buying, building, and franchising restaurants.

CHAPTER OUTLINE

Reasons to Open a Restaurant:
- Money
- The potential for a buy-out
- A place to socialize
- Love of a changing work environment
- Challenge
- Habit
- Too much time on your hands
- Opportunity to express yourself

French Culinary History
- 1767:
  - M. Boulanger:
    - The father of the modern restaurant.
    - Sold soups "restorantes" (restoratives).
    - Boulanger vs. the French Parliament.
    - The opening of Le Champ d' Oiseau.
- 1782:
  - Grand Tavern de Londres
  - Aux Trois Freres Provencaux
- 1794:
  - The French Revolution
    - Chefs to the former nobility suddenly had no employment.
    - Some chefs stayed and opened restaurants, some went to Europe; many chefs fled to America.

The Birth of Restaurants in America
- 1794:

- Paypalt brought the term restaurant to the United States.
- 1827:
    - Delmonico's, thought to be the first restaurant in America, opens.
        - Closed during the early years of Prohibition.

Challenges of Restaurant Operation
- Long hours
- Excessive fatigue can lead to health problems
- Little security for managers who work for others
- Family life can suffer
- For owner, possibility of losing investment and investors

Reasons for Restaurant Failure
- Lack of management traits/skills
- Lack of sufficient capital
- The expansion and competition from other restaurants
- Family problems

The Restaurant Failure Rate
- Results of Dr. Parsa's study:
    - Highest failure rate during first year- 26%
    - Second year- 19%
    - Third year- 14%
    - Failure rate of 59% for a three year period

Buy, Build, Franchise, or Manage?
- There are several career and investment options in the restaurant business:
    - Manage for someone else.
    - Purchase and operate a franchise.
    - Buy an existing restaurant and operate it as is or change its concept.
    - Build and operate a new restaurant.

Advantages of Buying
- Satisfies an aesthetic personal desire.
- High rewards if successful.
- Risks are somewhat reduced with knowledge of why the previous restaurant failed.

Disadvantages of Buying
- Difficult to overcome a poor reputation or poor location.
- High financial losses if restaurant fails:

- A fully equipped restaurant that seats 100 people costs anywhere from $6000 to $10,000 + per seat (or $600,000 to $1 million +) in addition to the site being bought or leased.
- In contrast, a sandwich shop can usually be opened for less than $30,000.

Advantages of Franchising
- Least financial risk (other than managing).

- Building design, menu, and marketing plans are already created and tested in market.

Quality Control
- Error detection, based on industrial systems, tends to be product oriented rather than service oriented.
- Critical in the restaurant business.
- All managers should carry a thermometer in their pocket so they can check that the food is being served at the correct temperature.

Starting from Scratch
- Would be restaurant operators come with a mix of different experiences in the business.
- The industry does not have nearly enough employees and turnover rate is high.
- The business is highly competitive, requires inordinate energy, the ability to work long hours and the willingness to accept a low salary!

Restaurants as Roads to Riches
- The most common reason people seek restaurant ownership is the possible financial rewards.

Practice Quiz

TRUE OR FALSE
On the following questions, answer whether the statement provided is true or false.

T   F   1. Delmonico's, located in New York City, is thought to be the first restaurant in America.

T   F   2. The first restaurant ever was called a "public dining room" and originated in France.

T   F   3. When opening a restaurant, one should never "borrow" ideas from existing restaurants.

T   F   4. Franchising and managing involve the least financial risk in that the restaurant format.

T   F   5. The restaurant industry currently has an overflow of employees.

T   F   6. A 100-seat restaurant, fully equipped, costs anywhere from $6,000 to $10,000 or more per seat.

T   F   7. The French Revolution in 1794 literally caused heads to roll, causing many chefs (to the former nobility) to become unemployed.

T   F   8. A sandwich shop can usually be opened for less than $15,000.

T   F   9. The biggest reason thousands of people seek restaurant ownership is the possible psychological rewards.

T   F   10. Emeril Lagasse thought to be the father of the modern restaurant.

FILL IN THE BLANKS: KEY TERM REVIEW

On the following questions, fill in the blank with the most appropriate key term.

1. A drink made from rum, beer, beaten eggs, and spices is called a _____.

2. The kind of restaurant _____ you select determines to a large extent the talents that will be required of employees.

3. A _____ includes building design, menu, and marketing plans, which already have been tested in the marketplace.

4. All managers should carry thermometers in their shirt pockets so they can check at any time that food is served at exactly the correct temperature. This is an example of _____.

5. M. Boulanger sold soups at his all-night tavern on the Rue Bailleul. He called these soups _____, which is the origin of the word restaurant.

MULTIPLE CHOICE QUESTIONS: CONCEPT REVIEW
On the following questions, circle the choice that best answers the question.

1. Which of the following individuals is thought to be the father of the modern restaurant?
   a. Parsa
   b. Boulanger
   c. Bailleul
   d. Delmonico

2.	Which of the following was located in New York City and is thought to be the first restaurant in America?
a. Delmonico's
b. Julian's Tavern
c. Grand Tavern
d. Julien's Restaurator

3.	Which of the following involves the least **financial** risk, yet the psychological risk may be high?
a. building
b. buying
c. managing
d. franchising

4.	Opening and operating a restaurant:
a. is fairly easy.
b. takes little money, if any at all.
c. is never a good idea.
d. takes dedication, high energy, ambition and persistence.

5.	A flip is made from:
a. vodka and orange juice.
b. rum, orange juice and cranberry juice.
c. rum, beer, beaten eggs, and spices.
d. vodka and eggnog.

6.	In working for others, managers have:
a. no job security.
b. little job security.
c. moderate job security.
d. a lot of job security.

7.	The term restaurant came to the United States in 1794, via a French refugee:
a. Boulanger.
b. Bailleul.
c. Delmonico.
d. Paypalt.

8.	Probably the biggest reason thousands of people seek restaurant ownership is the:
a. risk.
b. possible financial rewards.
c. challenge.
d. possible psychological rewards.

9.   A 100-seat restaurant, fully equipped, costs anywhere from:
      a. $1000 to $2000 per seat.
      b. $2000 to $3000 per seat.
      c. $5000 to $6000 per seat.
      d. $6,000 to $10,000 or more per seat.

10.   The first restaurant ever was called a:
      a. public dining room.
      b. private dining room.
      c. diner.
      d. public diner.

11.   A land marked study H.G. Parsa at Ohio State University found the actual failure rate of restaurants in Columbus, Ohio was:
      a. 59 percent for a three-year period.
      b. 19 percent for a three-year period.
      c. 80 percent for a three-year period.
      d. 10 percent for a three-year period.

12.   All managers should carry thermometers in their shirt pockets so they can check at any time that food is served at exactly the correct temperature. This is an example of:
      a. risk factors.
      b. a way to fire an employee.
      c. being over bearing.
      d. quality control.

13.   The successful restaurant owner is likely to:
      a. go out of business.
      b. be courted by a buyer.
      c. court a buyer.
      d. lose money.

14.   Boulanger believed that which of the following was the cure to all sorts of illnesses?
      a. vegetables
      b. carrot juice
      c. thyme
      d. soup

15.   Successful restaurants:
      a. can be highly profitable.
      b. are only moderately profitable.
      c. are not profitable.
      d. are never highly profitable.

SHORT ANSWER QUESTIONS

1. How did restaurants first come to America? _____

_____

_____

_____

2. Compare the advantages and disadvantages of **buying** a restaurant. _____

_____

_____

_____

3. Compare the advantages and disadvantages of **building** a restaurant. _____

_____

_____

_____

4. Compare the advantages and disadvantages of **franchising** a restaurant. _____

_____

_____

_____

5. Compare the advantages and disadvantages of **managing** a restaurant. _____

_____

_____

_____

CHAPTER 2: RESTAURANTS AND THEIR OWNERS

OBJECTIVES
- List and describe the various kinds and characteristics of restaurants.
- Compare and contrast chain, franchised and independent restaurant operations.
- Describe the advantages and disadvantages of Chef-Owned Restaurants.
- Define what a Centralized Home Delivery Restaurant is and what it offers.

CHAPTER OUTLINE

Chain or Independent
- Chain restaurants have some advantages and some disadvantages over independent restaurants.
- The advantages include: recognition in the marketplace, greater advertising clout, sophisticated systems development and discounted purchasing.
- Independent restaurants are relatively easy to open.
- The advantage for the independent restaurateur is that they can "do their own thing" in terms of concept development, menus, décor and so on.
- Some independent restaurants will grow into small chains and larger companies will buy them out.

Franchised
- Franchising involves the least risk:
    - Restaurant format, including building design, menu and marketing plans, have already been tested in the marketplace.
    - Less likely to go "belly up" than independent restaurants.
    - Training is provided.
    - Marketing and management supports are available.
- To open a franchise there is a franchising fee, a royalty fee, advertising royalty and requirements of substantial personal net worth.
- Franchisors help:
    - Site selection
    - Review of any proposed sites
    - Assist with design and building preparation
    - Help with preparation for opening
    - Train managers and staff
    - Plan and implement pre-opening marketing strategies
    - Conduct unit visits and provide on-going operating advice

Quick Service
- The Plate House, opened in the 1870's, was the 1st known quick-service restaurant.
- They served a quick lunch in about 10 minutes.
- Quick food production time is key.

- Many quick-service restaurants precook or partially cook food so that it can be finished off quickly
- The segment includes all restaurants where the food is paid for before service.
- Limited menus featuring burgers, chicken in many forms, tacos, burritos, hot dogs, fries, gyros, teriyaki bowels and so on.
- Goal is to serve maximum number of customers in minimum amount of time.

Fast Casual
- Defining traits are:
    - The use of high quality ingredients
    - Fresh made to order menu items
    - Healthy options
    - Limited or self-serving formats
    - Upscale décor
    - Carry-out meals

Bakery Café
- Mainly quick-service establishments.
- Different than a bakery in that they serve soups, salads and sandwiches.
- Many bake off goods that are prepared elsewhere or do final proofing after receiving goods.
- Many use central commissary systems.
- Variety of setting, products and ambiance.

Family
- Grew out of coffee shop style restaurant.
- Are frequently located in or within easy reach of the suburbs.
- Are informal with a simple menu and service designed to appeal to families.
- Some offer wine and beer but most offer no alcoholic beverages.

Casual
- Fits the societal trend of a more relaxed lifestyle.
- Defining factors include:
    - Signature food items
    - Creative bar menus or enhanced wine service'
    - A comfortable, homey décor'

Fine Dining
- Cuisine and service is expensive and leisurely.
- Very low table turnover (can be <1).
- Customers dine on special occasions and business relations.
- Usually proprietor- or partner-owned.
- Restaurants are small, usually less than 100 seats.

Fine Dining Economics
- Expensive, average check runs $60 or more

- High rent
- Large PR budgets
- High labor costs due to the necessity of highly experienced employees
- Much of the profits come from wine
- Tables, linen, dishes, décor very costly

Fine Dining Menus
- Expensive, imported items:
  - Foie Gras
  - Caviar
  - Truffles
- Presentation very important.
- Focus on visual, auditory and psychological experience.
- Extensive, expensive wine list.

Steak House
- Limited menu caters to a well-identified market.
- Service ranges from walk-up to high end.
- High food costs (as high as 50%) and low labor costs (as low as 12%).
- Majority of customers are men.

High-end operations:
- May have sales of $5 million or more per year
- Serve well-aged beef
- High percentage of wine and hard liquor sales

Low-end operations:
- Sales of $500,000 or less per year
- Beer and moderately priced wine

Types of Steak
- Steaks vary from a few ounces to 24 ounces!
- Tenderloin is most tender and runs along backbone.
- T-bone is cut from the small end of loin.
- Porterhouse contains T-bone and piece of tenderloin.
- New York Strip is a compact, dense, boneless cut of meat.
- Delmonico steak (or club steak) is a small, often boned steak, taken from the front section of the short loin.
- Sirloin steaks come from just in front of the round, between the rump and the shank.
- Wet aged: Meat that is wrapped in cryovac, sealed and refrigerated for several days.
- Dry aged: Takes place under a controlled temperature, humidity and airflow process that causes weight loss of 15% or more.

Seafood
- In Colonial America, seafood was a staple food in the taverns.
- Many seafood restaurants are owned and operated by independent restaurant owners.

- Red Lobster, with 677 restaurants, is the largest chain, with $2.5 billion in annual sales and average sales per restaurant of almost $3 million.
- Farm-bred fish is changing the cost and kind of fish that are readily available.
- French-farmed salmon, grown in pens, outnumber wild salmon from the ocean by 50 to 1.
- Seafood prices continue to rise but are in competition with shrimp grown in Mexico, India and Bangladesh.
- Aquaculture is predicted to grow and may bring the price of seafood down dramatically.

Ethnic
- Mexican:
    - Menu is often built around tortillas, ground beef, cilantro, chilies, rice and beans.
    - Relatively inexpensive because of the small percentage of meat used, which results in a food cost of less than 28% of sales.
    - Labor costs are also low because many of the employees are first-generation Americans or recent immigrants willing to work at minimum wage.
    - Menus, décor and music in Mexican restaurants are often colorful and exciting.

- Italian Restaurants
    - Italian restaurants, including pizza chains, boast the largest number of ethnic restaurants in the United States.
    - Offer an array of opportunities for would-be franchisees and entrepreneurs.
    - Owe their origins largely to poor immigrants from southern Italy, entrepreneurs who started small grocery stores, bars and restaurants in Italian neighborhoods.
    - Pizza is native to Naples and it was there that many American soldiers, during World War II, learned to enjoy it.

- Chinese Restaurants:
    - Represent a small percentage of all restaurants in America.
    - Historically, they are owned by hardworking ethnic Chinese families.
    - The cooking revolves around the wok, a large metal pan with a rounded bottom.
    - China is divided into culinary districts: Szechuan, Hunan, Cantonese and Northern style centered in Beijing.
    - Cantonese food is best known in the United States and Canada for its dim sum (small bites), steamed or fried dumplings stuffed with meat or seafood.
    - Szechuan food is distinguished by the use of hot peppers.
    - Chinese cooking styles reflect the places in China from which the chefs came.

Theme
- Built around an idea emphasizing fun and fantasy.
- Glamorize sports, travel, and eras in time.
- Celebrities are central to many theme restaurants (some are owners).
- Short life cycle compared to other types of popular restaurants.
- Do well outside major tourist attractions.
- Locals tire of the hype when food is often poor.
- Most of the profits come from merchandise not food sales.

- The cost of most of the large theme restaurants is high, both in capital costs and in operations.

Theme Categories
- Hollywood and the movies.
- Sports and sporting events.
- Time-the good old days.
- Travel-trains, planes and steamships.
- Ecology and the world around us.

Chef-Owned
- Part of American tradition of family restaurants.
- Publicity is key in gaining attention.
- One of the best-known husband-and-wife culinary team is Wolfgang Puck and Barbara Lazaroff.
  - Spago

Advantages:
- Having an experienced, highly motivated person in charge.
- Name often already known and synonymous with great food.
- Can be very profitable.

Disadvantages:
- Chefs often less knowledgeable about "the numbers".
- Can often make more money working as a chef in a name restaurant.
- Location and other factors are just as important for success as food preparation and presentation.

Women Chefs and Restaurant Owners
- The "typical" restaurant manager of the future may be a woman.
- Those with stamina and ambition may be better suited for management than are men with similar backgrounds.
- It is agreed that women are more concerned with details, sanitation and appearance.
- Women are more likely to be sensitive and empathetic with customers.

Centralized Home Delivery
- Centralization reduces the costs of order taking, food preparation, and accounting.
- Marketing costs may not decrease.
- Home delivery centers verify and process credit card information and use computers to perform the accounting.
- Order taking and accounting can be done at any location connected to the Internet, locally or internationally.
- The system does not even require that operators know what the customer has ordered; they simply transmit the order to a delivery person.

Practice Quiz

TRUE OR FALSE
On the following questions, answer whether the statement provided is true or false.

T   F   1.   The quick service restaurant segment includes all restaurants where food is paid for before service.

T   F   2.   Of the hundreds of types of ethnic restaurants in the United States, Mexican restaurants, boast the largest number.

T   F   3.   Franchising and managing involve the least financial risk in that the restaurant format.

T   F   4.   Centralization increases the costs of order taking, food preparation, and accounting.

T   F   5.   China is divided into culinary districts: Szechuan, Hunan, Cantonese and Northern style.

T   F   6.   Casual dining is less popular than the other types of restaurants because it does not fit the societal trends of a more relaxed lifestyle.

T   F   7.   Independent restaurants are relatively easy to open; all you need is a few thousand dollars, knowledge of restaurant operations and a strong desire to succeed.

T   F   8.   Fine dining refers to the cuisine and service provided in restaurants where food, drink, and service is expensive and usually leisurely.

T   F   9.   The first known quick- service restaurant dates back to the 1870s.

T   F 10.   Family restaurants grew out of the coffee shop style restaurant.

FILL IN THE BLANKS: KEY TERM REVIEW
On the following questions, fill in the blank with the most appropriate key term.

1.   Panera Bread Company and Au Bon Pain are the largest of the chain _____.

2.   With_____, an order for pizza could be processed in China and prepared for delivery in New York.

3.   One of the main advantages for opening a _____, is that the owner can "do their own thing" in terms of concept development, menus, décor and so on.

4.   The _____ segment includes all restaurants where the food is paid for before service.

5. _____ include a variety of specialized cuisines including Italian, Mexican, and Chinese.

6. Entry into the _____ category of restaurants is appealing to people who may wish to be part of a business that is simplified by a limited menu and that caters to a well-identified market—steak eaters.

7. Defining factors of a _____ include signature food items, creative bar menus or enhanced wine service, and comfortable, homey décor.

8. _____ are built around an idea, usually emphasizing fun and fantasy, glamorizing or romanticizing an activity such as sports, travel, and or a era in time.

9. _____ restaurants defining traits are; the use of high quality ingredients, fresh made to order menu items, healthful options, limited or self-serving formats, upscale décor and carryout meals.

10. _____ refers to the cuisine and service provided in restaurants where food, drink, and service is expensive and usually leisurely.

11. _____ restaurants possess the advantage of having an experienced, highly motivated person in charge.

12. _____ are frequently located in or within easy reach of the suburbs and are informal with a simple menu and service designed to appeal to families.

MULTIPLE CHOICE QUESTIONS
On the following questions, circle the choice that best answers the question.

1. Franchise restaurants are:
   a. more likely to go "belly up" than independent restaurants.
   b. more likely to close down willingly than independent restaurants.
   c. less likely to go "belly up" than independent restaurants.
   d. more risky than independent restaurants.

2. Which of the followings defining traits are: the use of high quality ingredients, fresh made to order menu items, healthful options, limited or self-serving formats, upscale décor and carryout meals?
   a. quick service
   b. fast casual
   c. casual
   d. dinner house

3. Meals are being ordered and delivered via the Internet in the same way as fresh flowers due to:
    a. centralization.
    b. DSL.
    c. phone lines.
    d. cable.

4. If you wish to be part of a business that is simplified by a limited menu and that caters to a **well-identified** market you may want to open a:
    a. quick service establishment.
    b. steakhouse.
    c. fine dining establishment.
    d. casual dining establishment.

5. Which of the following types of restaurants are built around an idea, usually emphasizing fun and fantasy, glamorizing or romanticizing an activity?
    a. Steakhouse
    b. Family
    c. Theme
    d. Seafood

6. Which of the following refers to the cuisine and service provided in restaurants where food, drink, and service are expensive and usually leisurely?
    a. bakery style restaurants
    b. fine dining style restaurants
    c. centralized style restaurants
    d. coffee shop style restaurants

7. Of the hundreds of types of ethnic restaurants in the United States, which type boasts the largest number?
    a. Seafood
    b. Mexican
    c. Chinese
    d. Italian

8. The QSR segment:
    a. includes all restaurants where the food is paid for before service.
    b. offers extensive menus.
    c. includes all restaurants where the food is paid after before service.
    d. includes steakhouses.

9. Independent restaurants are:
a. relatively easy to open, all you need is a few thousand dollars, knowledge of restaurant operations and a strong desire to succeed.
b. relatively hard to open, you need a lot of money, thousands of dollars, a knowledge of restaurant operations and a strong desire to succeed.
c. overall the most common type of restaurant.
d. very easy to open, you need no money, no knowledge of restaurant operations, but need a strong desire to succeed.

10. Which of the following is the largest seafood chain, with $2.5 billion in annual sales, average sales per restaurant of almost $3 million and 677 restaurants?
a. The Crab Shack
b. The Lobster Pot
c. Red Lobster
d. Shells

11. Which of the following types of steak is taken from the thick end of the short loin, has a T-bone and a sizable piece of tenderloin?
a. Porterhouse
b. Tenderloin
c. Prime Rib
d. New York Strip

12. Which of the followings defining factors include signature food items, creative bar menus, enhanced wine service, and comfortable, homey décor?
a. quick service restaurants
b. fine dining restaurants
c. casual dining restaurants
d. family restaurants

13. Family restaurants grew out of:
a. bakery style restaurants.
b. fine dining style restaurants.
c. centralized style restaurants.
d. coffee shop style restaurants.

14. The first known quick- service restaurant dates back to the 1870s, when a New York City foodservice establishment called the:
a. Plate House.
b. Grand Tavern.
c. Subway.
d. Delmonico's.

15. In the recent past, most food-service millionaires have been:
    a. managers.
    b. builders.
    c. buyers.
    d. franchisers.

SHORT ANSWER QUESTIONS

1. Name 3 advantages of opening a chain restaurant. _____

_____

_____

_____

2. Name 3 fast casual's defining traits and give several examples of fast casual restaurants. ____

_____

_____

_____

3. Explain an advantage of franchising a restaurant. _____

_____

_____

_____

4. Describe the advantages and disadvantages of chef-owned restaurants. _____

_____

_____

_____

5. Describe the advantages for independent restaurateurs. _____

_____

_____

_____

CHAPTER 3: CONCEPT, LOCATION, AND DESIGN

OBJECTIVES

- Recognize the benefits of a good restaurant name.

- Explain the relationship between concept and market.

- Explain why a restaurant concept might fail.

- Discuss some qualities of successful restaurant concepts.

- Identify factors to consider when choosing a restaurant's location.

- Identify factors to consider when developing a restaurant concept.

- List restaurant knockout criteria.

CHAPTER OUTLINE

Restaurant Concepts
- The matrix of ideas that constitute what will be perceived as the restaurant's image.
- It provides the framework on which to hang the image.
- Applies to any foodservice operation.
- Should fit a definite target market.
- Distinguishes the establishment as DandB, different and better, than the competition.
- May be necessary to modify as competition arises.

Symbols
- Aspects of the concept seen in the:
    - Sign
    - Logo
    - Colors
    - Upholstery
    - Food
    - Food presentation

Concepts: Clear Cut or Ambiguous?
- Many restaurants lack clear-cut concepts because there is no integration of the atmospherics.
- Everything should fit together:
    - Signs
    - Uniforms
    - Menus
    - Décor
- A concept is strengthened if it establishes an identity.

Protecting a Restaurant's Name
- Lawsuits happen!
- Trademark regulations protect the use of a name.
- If another party uses your name, you should take action.
- Loss of the right to a name means changing signs, menus, promotional material, etc.
- It also means the loss of power that has been built into the name by the superior operator.

Defining the Concept and Market
- In selecting a concept for a restaurant, define it precisely in the context of which markets will find it appealing.
- The market may constitute only a small percentage of the total population in an area.
  - i.e., A coffee shop with counter service would appeal to interstate travelers.
- Must be a market gap or need for the idea.

Successful Restaurant Concepts
- TGI Friday's has remained successful over the years because it has stayed close to the guest and concentrated on quality and service combined with a theme of fun.
- The Lettuce Entertain You Group has several theme restaurants in the Chicago area and beyond including:
  - Scoozi, which recalls an artist's studio and serves Italian country cuisine.
  - Café Ba-Ba-Reeba, a Spanish restaurant featuring tapas, the popular hot and cold "little dishes of Spain".
  - Shaw's Crab House, a premier seafood house features the Blue Crab Lounge—an oyster bar offering oysters on the half shell, clams, lobster, and crab dishes. The main dining room serves more than 40 fresh seafood items plus chicken and beef.
- Hard Rock Café
- Union Square Café
- Corner Bakery Café

Concept Adaptation
- Most concepts that have not been tested need some adaptation to the particular market.
- Concept development has always been important in the restaurant industry, but it is becoming more so now that *dining districts* are developing in almost every community.
- Different menus and prices attract different markets.

Changing/Modifying a Concept
- Many highly successful concepts that have worked well for years gradually turn sour.
  - The customer base and the demographics change.
  - Morale and personal service may decline.
- Copy and improve
  - There is no such thing as a completely new restaurant concept—only modifications, changes, new combinations, changes in design, layout, menu, and service.

Restaurant Symbology
- Restaurant symbology includes the logo, the line drawings, the linen napkins and the service uniforms.
- This all helps to create the atmosphere.
    - Cesar Ritz: Waiters dressed in tails.
    - Chart House: Servers dressed in Hawaiian attire.
    - McDonald's: Ronald McDonald.

When a Concept Fails
- The concept can be changed to fit the market.
- Conversion from one concept to another can take place while the restaurant is doing business.
- A new concept (complete with decor, price, and service), may better appeal to the same market and siphon customers away from the competition.

The Multiple-Concept Chain
- Multiple-concept restaurant chains can have five or more restaurants in the same block, each competing with the others, each acquiring a part of the restaurant market.
- Customers do not like feeling like they are eating in the same restaurant all over the area, so the restaurants are varied somewhat and carry different names.
- The largest of all restaurant companies, Tricon Global Restaurants, Inc., has three concepts—KFC, Taco Bell, and Pizza Hut. They stand alone, twin or even triple concepts.

Sequence of Restaurant Development
1. Business marketing initiated
2. Layout and equipment planned
3. Menu determined
4. First architectural sketches made
5. Licensing and approvals sought
6. Financing arranged
7. Working blueprints developed
8. Contracts for bidding
9. Contractor selected
10. Construction or remodeling begun
11. Furnishing and equipment ordered
12. Key personnel hired
13. Hourly employees selected and trained
14. Restaurant opened

Planning Services
- Many aspects of restaurant design are carried out by other parties, hired by the owners and management. The designer, for example, performs the following services:
    - Basic floor plan
    - Equipment schedule
    - Electrical requirements

- Plumbing requirements
- Equipment
- Equipment elevations
- Refrigeration requirements
- Exhaust and in-take requirements

Common Denominators
- Some factors may be common to all kinds of restaurants.

Profitability
- Most profitable restaurants are in quick-service category because they have:
  - Predominantly minimum-wage personnel
  - High sales volume
  - The use of systems
  - Excellent marketing

The Mission Statement
- The purpose of the business and the nature of what it offers.
- The business goals, objectives, and strategies.
- Philosophies and values the business and employees follow.

Location and Design
- Demographics of the area: age, occupation, religion, nationality, race, family size, educational level, average income of individuals and families.
- Visibility from a major highway.
- Accessibility from a major highway.
- Number of potential customers passing by the restaurant (potential customers might be only travelers going through a community, drivers, local workers).
- Distance from the potential market.
- Desirability of surroundings.
- Dinner or family-style restaurants need not place the same high priority on convenience of location necessary for casual and quick-service establishments
- Location decisions are based on asking the right questions and securing the right information.
- Real estate agents are prime sources.
- Other sources of information are the chamber of commerce, banks, town or city planners and other restaurant operators.
- Town and city planning officials can provide traffic and zoning information. Know what zoning officials are planning for the future.
- Locations wax and wane in desirability, depending on a number of conditions, including the general economy, the nature of the residents of the area, the presence or absence of new or declining buildings, changing traffic flows and security.
- Look for built-in traffic generators such as hotels, business parks, ballparks, indoor arenas, theaters, retail centers and residential neighborhoods.

Location Criteria
- Proper zoning.
- Drainage, sewage, utilities.
- Minimal size.
- Length of lease.
- Excessive traffic speed.
- Access from a highway or street.
- Visibility from both sides of the street.
- Market population.
- Family income.
- Growth or decline of the area.
- Competition from comparable restaurants.
- The restaurant row or cluster concept.

Visibility and Design Criteria
- Visibility and accessibility are important criteria for any restaurant.
    - Visibility is the extent to which the restaurant can be seen for a reasonable amount of time, whether the potential guest is walking or driving.

- Design needs to correlate with the theme and includes:
    - Space allocation - front of the house and backstage
    - Lighting (single most important element)
    - Color (in tandem with lighting)
    - Layout of the dining area

Practice Quiz

TRUE OR FALSE
On the following questions, answer whether the statement provided is true or false.

T   F   1. Concept comprises everything that affects how the patron views the restaurant: public relations, advertising, promotion, and the operation itself.

T   F   2. Concept development has always been important in the restaurant industry, but it is becoming more so now that dining districts are developing in almost every community.

T   F   3. Loss of the right to use a name means changing signs, menus, and promotional material.

T   F   4. If the operator is competent, they should sell their restaurant if it is failing.

T   F   5. Turnover is slightly correlated with the efficiency of the operation.

T   F   6. There is no such thing as a completely new restaurant concept.

T F 7. Up to 75 percent of the meals eaten away from home are for utilitarian purposes, while the other 25 percent are for pleasure.

T F 8. McDonald's is a multiple concept chain.

T F 9. You should never name a restaurant after its owner.

T F 10. The best guide in selecting a planner/consultant is that person's experience and reputation.

KEY TERM FILL IN THE BLANKS: KEY TERM REVIEW
On the following questions, fill in the blank with the most appropriate key term.

T F 1. Using a town or city map and plotting the location of existing restaurants on the map, is an example of a _____.

T F 2. The _____ includes everything that affects how the patrons will view the restaurant.

T F 3. A _____ should include a vision of what the restaurant owner would like for the restaurant in the future.

T F 4. If another party uses your restaurant name, you should _____, take action against that person by proving that you, the challenging party, used the name first.

T F 5. When opening a new restaurant you should try to develop a concept better suited to its market than that presented by competing restaurants. This is known as being _____.

T F 6. From the time a concept is put together, until a location is obtained, there is a _____.

T F 7. Without a doubt, the most _____ restaurants are in quick-service category.

T F 8. The _____ offered probably correlates with menu price and pleasure—at least, that is the expectation of the diner.

MULTIPLE CHOICE QUESTIONS: CONCEPT REVIEW

On the following questions, circle the choice that best answers the question.

1. The best concepts are often the result of:
    a. learning from mistakes.
    b. franchising.
    c. building new.
    d. managing.

2. People often spend about _____ minutes travel time when going to a cafeteria or department store restaurant.
    a. 5
    b. 10
    c. 15
    d. 20

3. A concept created by Lettuce Entertain You Enterprises is:
    a. Papagus.
    b. Corner Bakery Café.
    c. Hard Rock Café.
    d. Automat.

4. Concepts comprise:
    a. advertising only.
    b. everything that affects how the patron views the restaurant.
    c. promotion only.
    d. everything that affects how the worker views the restaurant.

5. The best guide in selecting a planner/consultant is that persons:
    a. demeanor.
    b. way of dressing.
    c. experience and reputation.
    d. overall appearance.

6. Up to ___ percent of the meals eaten away from home are for utilitarian purposes, while the other ___ percent are for pleasure.
    a. 75, 25
    b. 90, 10
    c. 25, 75
    d. 10, 90

7. Surveys show that 40 to 50 percent of all table-service restaurant customers arrive in:
    a. groups of 4.
    b. groups of 3 or more.
    c. pairs.
    d. singles.

8. Symbols are:
   a. seen in the sign, logo, colors, upholstery, and lighting of the restaurant.
   b. not seen in the sign, logo, colors, upholstery, and lighting of the restaurant.
   c. are not part of the concept.
   d. are not used in developing a restaurant.

9. Without a doubt, the most profitable restaurants are in the:
   a. steak house category.
   b. fast food category.
   c. fine dining category.
   d. quick service category.

10. The magazine *Restaurant Business* publishes an annual *Restaurant Growth Index*, the purpose of which is to list:
    a. all the new restaurants that opened in the United States.
    b. the best and worst places to open a restaurant in the United States.
    c. new restaurant job openings.
    d. all the new restaurants that opened in the major cities of the United States.

11. Which of the following is the prime source of information for restaurant location decisions?
    a. banks
    b. the IRS
    c. real estate agents
    d. newspapers

12. Generally, restaurant patrons will travel an average of ___ to ___ minutes to reach a hotel, steak, full-menu, or fish restaurant.
    a. 5 to 10
    b. 11 to 15
    c. 15 to 18
    d. 18 to 25

13. The logo, the line drawings, even the linen napkins and the service uniforms are all part of:
    a. restaurant symbology.
    b. the market.
    c. why a concept fails.
    d. visibility.

14. Concept development has always been important in the restaurant industry, it is now becoming:
    a. less so in todays market.
    b. more so now that dining districts are developing in almost every community.
    c. nearly impossible due to the population explosion.
    d. impossible to do since the market is always changing.

15. The name of the restaurant is:
    a. really not important if the concept is defined.
    b. not part of the image.
    c. should be very descriptive.
    d. part of the image.

SHORT ANSWER QUESTIONS

1. What is the 14-step sequence of restaurant development? _____

_____

_____

_____

_____

_____

_____

_____

_____

_____

2. Name 5 services a designer performs. _____

_____

_____

_____

3. Describe 3 reasons the most profitable restaurants are in the quick-service category? _____

_____

_____

_____

4. Name 7 "knockout criteria" for selecting a location. _____

_____

_____

_____

CHAPTER 4: BUSINESS AND MARKETING PLANS

OBJECTIVES

- Identify the major elements of a business plan.

- Develop a restaurant business plan.

- Conduct a market assessment.

- Discuss the importance of the four P's of the marketing mix.

- Describe some promotional ideas for a restaurant.

CHAPTER OUTLINE

The Business Plan
- Increases the probability of success.
- Assists in obtaining financing.
- Communicates to potential investors.
- Defines operational purpose.
- Mission statements generally do not change.
- Goals are reviewed as often as necessary.
- Goals should be established for each key operational area (e.g., sales, food, service, beverage, labor costs, etc.).
- Strategies or action plans are the "how to reach the goal." They are more specific than goals and are generally short-term.
- Strategies are specific as to the date by which they are to be achieved and how much should be achieved.
- Based on strategies, a detailed action plan with individual responsibilities should be implemented.

The Elements of a Business Plan
- Cover sheet
- Description of the business
- Description of the concept licenses and lease
- Market analysis and strategy
- Financial Data
- Appendices

The Difference Between Marketing and Sales
- Sales focus on the needs of the seller.
- Marketing focuses on the needs of the buyer.

Marketing

- Restaurant marketing is based on a marketing philosophy.
- Marketing philosophy patterns the way management and ownership have decided to relate to guests, employees, purveyors and the general public in terms of fairness, honesty and moral conduct.
- Marketing is finding out what guests want and providing it at a fair price.
- Includes sales and merchandising.
- Determines who will patronize the restaurant and what they want in it.
- Is an ongoing effort.
- Gets into psyche of present and potential patrons.
- Marketing is about solving guest problems.

Sales

- A part of marketing that focuses on the needs of the seller.
- Activities that stimulate the patron to want what the restaurant offers.
- The actions of restaurant employees that influence patrons after they have arrived at the restaurant.
- Sales mentality exists when seller thinks only of his or her needs and pushes an item on a customer.
- Closely related to advertising, promotion and public relations.

Marketing Planning and Strategy

- Every marketing plan must have realistic goals for guest satisfaction, market share, sales and costs while leaving a reasonable profit margin.
- SWOT analysis, stands for strengths, weaknesses, opportunities and threats.

Market Assessment, Demand, Potential and Competition Analysis
Market Assessment

- Analyzes the community, the potential guests, the competition and helps to answer the all-important questions:
- Is there a need for a restaurant?
- Who will be the potential guests?

Market Demand

- The demand for a restaurant is calculated using two factors:
- The population in the catchment area (the area around the restaurant from which people would normally be drawn to the restaurant).
- The demographic split of this population by nationality, race, age, sex, religion, employment, education, and income.

Market Segmentation

- The market—that is, the total of all actual and potential guests—is generally segmented into groups of buyers with similar characteristics.
- Within these groups are target markets, which are groups identified as the best ones for the restaurant to serve.

Typical Market Segmentation
- Geographic
- Demographic
- Behavior

Competition Analysis
- Analyzing the competition's strengths and weaknesses helps in formulating marketing goals and strategies to use in the **marketing action plan.**
- When analyzing the competition it makes sense to do a **comparison benefit matrix** showing how your restaurant compares to the competition.
- You choose the items for comparison, which include name recognition, ease of access, parking, curbside appeal, greeting, holding area, seating, ambiance, food, service, cleanliness, value, and so on...

Marketing Mix-The 4 P's
- Place
- Product
- Price
- Promotion

Practice Quiz

TRUE OR FALSE
On the following questions, answer whether the statement provided is true or false.

T   F   1. Marketing focuses on the needs and wants of guests.

T   F   2. Public relations are efforts to make the public favor the restaurant without resorting to paid advertising.

T   F   3. Most operators price the more expensive items using the cost-based method.

T   F   4. Business plans begin with a market analysis and strategy, which outlines the elements of the plan.

T   F   5. The mission of a restaurant is reviewed and changed as often as necessary.

T   F   6. Price is the only revenue-generating variable in the marketing mix.

T   F   7. Sales focus on the needs and wants of the guests.

T   F   8. Today, restaurateurs are placing less emphasis on atmospherics and more emphasis on low pricing.

T   F   9. Advertising is purchased in newspapers, radio, TV, and/or similar businesses.

T   F   10. The main components of the marketing plan are known as the four Ps: product, place, promotion, and price.

FILL IN THE BLANKS: KEY TERM REVIEW
On the following questions, fill in the blank with the most appropriate key term.

1.   Restaurateurs are placing greater emphasis on_____, the design used to create a special atmosphere.

2.   Before embarking on the complex task of setting up any business, especially a restaurant, it is essential to do a _____, which will help increase the probability of success for the restaurant.

3.   _____ are the "how to reach the goal," are more specific than goals, and are generally short-term.

4.   Once the target market is identified, it is important to _____ the restaurant to stand out from the competition, and to focus on advertising and promotional messages to guests.

5.   Restaurant product can be described as having three_____: the core product, the formal product, and the augmented product

6.   _____ calculates the cost of the ingredients and multiplies it by a factor of 3 to obtain a food cost percentage of 33.

7.   Restaurants, like all businesses, go through a _____from introduction to decline; the trick is to extend the stages.

8.   _____ implies determining who will patronize a restaurant and what they want in it—its design, atmosphere, menu, and service.

9.   _____ conveys to the customer the best face or image of the restaurant, what people like most about it, or how it stands out from the competition

10.   Restaurant owners usually want their restaurant to be different in one or more ways, to call attention to the food or ambiance, this is known as _____.

11.   _____, which includes communication, seeks to inform and persuade customers.

12.   The _____, that is the total of all actual and potential guests, is generally _____ into groups of buyers with similar characteristics.

13. Food and labor costs, when added together, are known as _____.

14. _____ covers the quality, pricing, and service of the product offered.

15. Restaurant marketing is based on a _____, which patterns the way management and owners have decided to relate to guests, employees, purveyors, and the general public.

MULTIPLE CHOICE QUESTIONS: CONCEPT REVIEW
On the following questions, circle the choice that best answers the question.

1. Which of the following is finding out what guests want and providing it at a fair price that leaves a reasonable profit?
   a. Positioning
   b. Segmenting
   c. Sales
   d. Marketing

2. According to the text, the total of all actual and potential guests is called the:
   a. buyers.
   b. pool.
   c. market.
   d. none of the above.

3. One marketing technique is the SWOT analysis, it stands for:
   a. strengths, weaknesses, opportunities and threats.
   b. segmenting, weaning, optimizing, training.
   c. strengths, weaning, optimizing, training.
   d. segmenting, weaning, opportunities and threats.

4. Which of the following are the three typical market segmentations?
   a. Geographic, Demographic, Behavior
   b. Demographic, Behavior, Style
   c. Concept, Geographic, Demographic
   d. Behavior, Concept, Geographic

5. The only revenue-generating variable in the marketing mix is:
   a. Place.
   b. Product Life Cycle.
   c. Positioning.
   d. Price.

6. Which of the following conveys to the customer the best face or image of the restaurant, what people like most about it, or how it stands out from the competition?
   a. Differentiation

b. Positioning
c. Place
d. Product Life Cycle

7. Restaurant product can be described as having which of the following product levels?
a. core product
b. formal product
c. augmented product
d. all the above

8. When analyzing the competition it makes sense to do a _____, which shows how your restaurant compares to the competition.
a. market segmentation
b. reality benefit analysis
c. guest potential matrix
d. comparison benefit matrix

9. The conventional-wisdom method of pricing, which calculates the cost of the ingredients and multiplies it by a factor of 3, to obtain a food cost percentage of 33, is called:
a. cost-based pricing.
b. competitive pricing.
c. contribution pricing.
d. a and c.

10. Food and labor costs, when added together, are known as:
a. prime costs.
b. competitive costs.
c. variable costs.
d. fixed costs.

11. The cover sheet of a business plan should have the:
a. name of the business.
b. the owner's name and associates' names.
c. current or proposed address.
d. all the above.

12. A part of marketing that focuses on the needs of the seller is called:
a. assessment.
b. sales.
c. demand.
d. analysis.

13. The key to positioning is:
a. how employees perceive the restaurant.
b. how guests perceive the restaurant.
c. the amount of guests that come to the restaurant.

d. employee training.

14. Demographics include:
    a. age, sex, family life cycle, income, and occupation, education, religion, and race.
    b. country, state/province, county, city, and neighborhood.
    c. occasions, benefits sought, user status, usage rates, loyalty status, and buyer readiness stage.
    d. all the above.

15. A market assessment analyzes the:
    a. community.
    b. potential guests.
    c. competition.
    d. all the above

SHORT ANSWER QUESTIONS

1. Name 3 benefits of creating a business plan. _____

_____

_____

_____

2. What are the differences between sales and marketing? _____

_____

_____

_____

3. What information will be gained from completing a marketing assessment? _____

_____

_____

_____

4. Name the 3 most common areas of market segmentation? _____

_____

_____

_____

5. What are the 4 P's of the marketing mix? _____

_____

_____

_____

CHAPTER 5: FINANCING AND LEASING

OBJECTIVES

- Forecast restaurant sales.

- Prepare an income statement and a financial budget.

- Identify requirements for obtaining a loan in order to start a restaurant.

- Discuss the strengths and weaknesses of the various types of loans available to restaurant operators.

- List questions and the types of changes a lessee should consider before signing a lease.

- Discuss the strengths and weaknesses of the various types of loans available to restaurant operators.

CHAPTER OUTLINE

Sufficient Capital
- Many would-be restaurateurs try to start restaurants with only a few thousand dollars in capital. Such ventures usually fail.
- Lack of finance and working capital is a close second to lack of management when it comes to reasons for restaurant failure.
- Working capital is the standby amount of cash to open the restaurant and get through possibly several unprofitable months of operation.
- Commercial banks are a common source of funds.

Preparing for the Loan Application
- Aspiring restaurateurs have bought the furniture and fixtures of an existing restaurant for $30,000.
- This money is paid to the previous person leasing the property, for the work they had done to set up a restaurant, including the kitchen, storeroom, toilets, dining area, plumbing and electrical.
- This $30,000 was paid after a due diligence—a thorough check to assure that everything works and that the health department or some other agency is not about to shut the place down for some infringement of their regulations.
- Larger restaurants will naturally cost more to get into, and it is just a matter of finding a location and price that are right for you.

Budgeting
- The purpose of budgeting is to "do the numbers" and more accurately forecast if the restaurant will be viable.
- Sales must cover all costs, including interest on loans, and allow for reasonable profit, greater than if the money were successfully invested in stocks, bonds, or real estate.
- Financial lenders require budget forecasts as a part of the overall business plan.

Forecasting Sales
- Sales forecasting for a restaurant is, at best, calculated guesswork.
- Many factors beyond the control of the restaurant, such as unexpected economic factors and weather affect sales.
- Without a fairly accurate forecast of sales, it is impossible to predict the success or failure of the restaurant because all expenses, fixed and variable are dependent on sales for payment.
- Sales volume has two components: the average guest checks and guest counts.
- The average guest check is the total sales divided by the number of guests.
- The totals from each of the accounting periods add up to a yearly total sales forecast.
- The sales forecast for the first few months should consider the facts that it takes time for people to realize that the restaurant is open and that a large number of people are usually attracted to a new restaurant.

Budgeting Costs
- Two main cost categories:
    - Variable:
        - Change proportionately according to sales.
    - Fixed:
        - Unaffected by changes in sales volume.

Uniform System of Accounts for Restaurants
- Outlines uniform classifications and presentations of operating results.
- Allows for easier comparisons to foodservice industry statistics.
- Provides a turnkey accounting system.
- Is a time-tested system.

Productivity Analysis and Costs Control
- Various measures of productivity have been developed:
- The simplest employee productivity measure is sales generated per employee per year.

Securing a Loan
- Compare Interest Rates
    - A difference of 1 % over a period of years is big money!
- Beware of bankers who demand:
    - Interest discounted in advance:
        - Borrower pays interest on a lower amount than was actually received.

    - Compensating balance:
        - Banker requires a certain amount to remain in the bank at all times.

Real Interest Rates
- The interest deductions allowable by the Internal Revenue Service (IRS) cut the real cost of a loan considerably.
- The higher the tax bracket, the lower the net cost of the interest paid.

Small Business Administration
- User-friendly.
- Excellent record of success in lending money to restaurants.
- 3 Principal Parties:
    - SBA.
    - The small business borrower.
    - The private lender.
- The lender plays the central role.
- Government cosigns loan.
- SBA loans have four basic requirements:
    1. The right type of business.
    2. A clear idea of which loan program is best for you.
    3. Knowing how to fill out the application properly.
    4. The willingness to provide the detailed financial and market data required.

SBICS
- Independently owned and managed companies set up to provide debt and equity capital to small businesses.
- Minorities Enterprise SBICs, specialize in loans to minority-owned firms.
- Amounts loaned range from $20,000 to $1 million or more.

Service Corps of Retired Executives
- Made up of successful retired businesspeople who work on a volunteer basis to help businesses with specific problems.
- SCORE executives who are experts in disciplines such as accounting, layout, food purchasing, menu planning and so on can be requested.
    - Their services are provided at no charge.

Collateral
- Collateral is:
    - Security for the lender.
    - Personal property or other possessions the borrower assigns to the lender as a pledge of debt repayment.
- If debt is not repaid, the lender becomes owner of the collateral.
- Character of the applicant is the most important type of collateral.
- Collateral accepted by banks:
    - Real estate
    - Stocks and bonds
    - Chattel mortgages
    - Life insurance
    - Assignment of lease
    - Savings account
    - Endorsers/Co-makers/Guarantors

Leasing
- Restaurant buildings and equipment are more likely to be leased than purchased by the beginner because less capital is required for leasing than for building or buying.
- The signer is obligated to pay for the entire lease period.
- A restaurant lease should be good for both parties—the landlord (lesser) and the tenant (lessee).
- Beginners should try for a 5 year lease with an option to renew for several additional 5 year periods.
- Leases generally, depending on location, approximate 5 to 8% of sales, but can go as high as 12%.
- Lease costs are calculated on a square-foot basis, with charges ranging from $2 to $50 per square foot per month, depending on the location.
- In making a lease, both parties should consult a lawyer versed in real estate terminology to avoid misunderstandings.

What is a Restaurant Worth?
- 2 Potential Values:
  - Real estate value.
    - Usually determined by competitive values in the community.
    - Market value of real estate tends to follow the value set by similar properties in the area.
  - Value as a profit generator.

Practice Quiz

TRUE OR FALSE
On the following questions, answer whether the statement provided is true or false.

T   F   1. Commercial banks take more risks than other lending facilities because they have the largest pool of money to draw from.

T   F   2. Due diligence is a thorough check to assure that everything works and that the health department is not about to shut the place down for some infringement of their regulations.

T   F   3. Fixed costs change proportionately according to sales.

T   F   4. The rapid-turnover style of restaurant generally has a high check average, but produce a low sales volume.

T   F   5. Controllable expense is the term used to describe the expenses that cannot be changed in the short term.

T   F   6. Commercial banks are common sources of funds that people go to when opening a new restaurant.

38

T F 7. Variable costs are normally unaffected by changes in sales volume—that is, they do not change significantly with changes in business performance.

T F 8. The purpose of budgeting is to "do the numbers" and, more accurately, forecast if the restaurant will be viable.

T F 9. In order to obtain a bank loan you will often need to prove that you have the funds to pay mortgage insurance, taxes, the required down payment, and closing costs.

T F 10. Lack of finance and working capital is a close second to lack of management when it comes to reasons for restaurant failure.

FILL IN THE BLANKS: KEY TERM REVIEW
On the following questions, fill in the blank with the most appropriate key term.

1. The borrower should not wait to request a loan until just before it is needed. They should begin to _____ as soon as possible.

2. The standby amount of cash to open the restaurant, and to get through possibly several unprofitable months of operation, is called _____.

3. A clumsy or slow waitperson is a _____ in an operation that depends on turnover for sales volume.

4. _____ specializes in loans to minority-owned firms.

5. Restaurant buildings and equipment are more likely to be _____ by the beginner because less capital is required.

6. When the banker requires a certain amount to remain in the bank at all times this is called a _____.

7. The _____ organization is made up of successful retired businesspeople who work on a volunteer basis to help businesses with specific problems.

8. _____ are independently owned and managed companies set up to provide debt and equity capital to small businesses.

9. When operators or would-be restaurateurs have a choice of lenders, they should, by all means, compare _____.

10. Forms of _____ are the assets that the bank can take should the loan not be repaid.

MULTIPLE CHOICE QUESTIONS: CONCEPT REVIEW
On the following questions, circle the choice that best answers the question.

1. Sales forecasting for a restaurant is:
    a. calculated guesswork.
    b. exact science.
    c. calculated science.
    d. unnecessary.

2. The number-one factor in restaurant failure is said to be:
    a. lack of promotion.
    b. lack of capital.
    c. lack of management.
    d. lack of employees.

3. Costs that are normally unaffected by changes in sales volume are called:
    a. variable.
    b. uncontrolled.
    c. fixed.
    d. none of the above.

4. There is a ___ percent success rate of the SBA loans to restaurants.
    a. 25
    b. 55
    c. 45
    d. 65

5. Which of the following is not a source of collateral for a bank mentioned in the text?
    a. Real estate
    b. Savings accounts
    c. Life insurance
    d. Automobiles

6. Loans cannot be made at more than _____ percent interest over the prime lending rate.
    a. 2.25
    b. 2.50
    c. 2.75
    d. 3.00

7. Single-use real estate loans typically run less than:
    a. 20 years.
    b. 25 years.
    c. 30 years.
    d. 55 years.

8. A term loan is one repaid in installments, usually over a period longer than _____.
   a. 5 years
   b. 1 year
   c. 10 years
   d. 15 years

9. A standby amount of cash to open the restaurant and to get through possibly several unprofitable months of operation is called:
   a. capital.
   b. profit.
   c. collateral.
   d. income.

10. Expenses that can be changed in the short term are called:
    a. uncontrollable.
    b. controllable.
    c. fixed.
    d. a and c.

11. The banker requires a certain amount to remain in the bank at all times. This is called having a:
    a. retreating discount.
    b. advanced discount.
    c. compensating balance.
    d. assessment balance.

12. Costs that change proportionately according to sales are called:
    a. variable.
    b. controlled.
    c. fixed.
    d. none of the above.

13. Intermediate loans are made for up to:
    a. 20 years.
    b. 15 years.
    c. 10 years.
    d. 5 years.

14. Banks want assets that they can take if a loan is not repaid, this is called:
    a. swindling.
    b. collateral.
    c. negotiating.
    d. capital.

15. Lending officers:
    a. maximize risks.
    b. are largely judge on the amount of loans they approve.
    c. tend to be ultraconservative.
    d. tend to be negligent.

SHORT ANSWER QUESTIONS

1. A restaurant has two potential values: its real estate value and its value as a profit generator. Explain the difference between the two. _____

   _____

   _____

   _____

   _____

   _____

2. A hypothetical restaurant is a space of 8,000 square feet leased at $8 per square foot. The monthly rent would be: _____

   _____

   _____

3. The annual rent for the above restaurant would be: _____

   _____

   _____

4. Why are restaurant buildings and equipment more likely to be leased than purchased by the beginner? _____

   _____

   _____

   _____

   _____

   _____

CHAPTER 6: LEGAL AND TAX MATTERS

OBJECTIVES

- Describe the various forms of business ownership.

- Discuss the advantages and disadvantages of each form of business.

- Recognize the legal aspects of doing business.

- Discuss various types of government regulations.

CHAPTER OUTLINE

What Business Entity is the Best?
- Types of entities:
  - Sole proprietorship
  - Partnership
  - Corporation
- Under the law, all businesses are operated as proprietorships, partnerships, or corporations.
- Business ventures have a choice of these entities, each with different tax consequences, advantages and disadvantages.

Sole Proprietorship
- Individual Ownerships.
- As sole proprietor, the restaurant operator does not draw a salary for federal income tax purposes.
  - He or she reports as income the profit for the year or deducts, as an expense, any loss for the year.
- For tax purposes, the proprietor is not an employee; however, his or her income is subject to self-employment tax.
- Advantages:
  - It is simple.
  - Reasonable salary.
  - Funds can be withdrawn without any tax consequences.
  - Business can be discontinued or sold with minimal tax consequences.
- Disadvantages:
  - The owner cannot be a participant in the company's qualified pension and/or profit sharing plans.
  - The owner is liable for every aspect of the business including debts.
  - No legal existence apart from the owner or owners.

The Partnership
- Any venture where 2 or more persons endeavor to make a profit.
- General partnerships: Complete liability but full management rights.
- Limited partnerships: Share limited liability with no services performed.
- Advantages:
  - Can be quite flexible.
  - No double taxation.
  - Choice of limited or general partnership.
  - Allows flexibility.
- Disadvantages:
  - Same problems of legal liability as the sole proprietorship.
  - Ability of a partner to create debts for the partnership.
  - In bad times, partners always see the other as at fault.
  - Difficult to divide assets if business fails.
  - Can be expected to dissolve eventually.
  - Death, disagreement and/or ill health can make perfection into a nightmare!

The Corporation
- A legal entity similar to a person, in that it can borrow, buy, conduct business and must pay state and federal taxes on profits.
- Deciding whether to incorporate can often depend on the amount of insurance coverage available.
- Advantages:
  - Limited liability.
  - Ease of availability and affordability of insurance through group plans.
  - Corporate fringe benefits are available.
  - Can sell and distribute stock.
  - Investor friendly.
- Disadvantages:
  - Double taxation.
  - Takes a lot of money to set up.
  - Usually requires legal and accounting advice, which can be costly.
  - Can lose control if too much stock is distributed.

The S Corporation
- Permits the business entity to operate as a corporation but allows it to avoid paying corporation taxes.
- Avoids a double tax upon liquidation due to built-in gains from appreciation of assets.
- Useful for a family restaurant.
- Ideal if owners do not want to accumulate after-tax income in the corporation or if shareholders are in a low tax bracket.
- Provides tax advantages for dependent children or parents.
- Corporation taxes are avoided and profits from the restaurant are taxed according to income brackets.
- IRS requires that corporate officers draw a fair salary so that the company's earnings are not overstated.

- Benefits of more than 2% of annual salary cannot be deducted.

Buy-sell Agreements
- In the sale of a business, a buy-sell agreement preserves continuity of ownership in the business.
- A buy-sell agreement is made up of several legal clauses in a business that can control the following business decisions:
    - Who can buy a departing partner's or shareholder's share of the business.
    - What events will trigger a buyout.
    - What price will be paid for a partner's share.

Depreciation and Cash Flow
- As a business generates income and pays immediate expenses, including taxes, the money left over is not all profit.
- In a restaurant, the building, kitchen equipment, dining room equipment and furnishings depreciate year after year, until finally they have no value or only a salvage value.
- Theoretically, money is set aside for replacing these items—a depreciation allowance.
- Actually, this money is seldom set aside and very often, the building, instead of depreciating in value, appreciates.

Retirement Tax Shelters
- The individual retirement annuity (IRA) and the Keogh plans:
    - Makes it possible for a self-employed person or someone who has income from self-employment to put up to $30,000 per year or 25% of the annual income from the self-employment into a tax-sheltered retirement plan.
    - The earnings from money generated in a retirement plan are deferred from taxes.
    - For either plan, the money can be managed through a custodian as directed by the person having the account.

Business Expenses and Taxes
- Anything that is a cost of doing business is tax deductible (if the IRS agrees).
    - For example, a restaurant operator attends the National Restaurant Show held in Chicago. All expenses are tax deductible.
- The list of fringe benefits that are legitimate for tax purposes is extensive and imaginative.

Local, State and Federal Taxes
- One of the most onerous of the operator's tasks is keeping records and submitting tax reports.
- The operator not only pays taxes as required on restaurant sales but also is responsible for collecting and paying taxes to the city, state, and federal governments.
- Workers' compensation insurance is federally mandated but administered by the states.
- Every business with at least 1 employee in addition to the owner, must register with the IRS, acquire an employer identification number and withhold federal payroll taxes from employees' pay.

Legal Aspects of Contract Services
- Restaurant operators often contract out services such as air-conditioning repairs, maintenance, janitorial services, and pest control.
- Independent contractors have proved popular because they are skilled in their field and the restaurant operator avoids the liabilities for unemployment insurance, workers' compensation, wrongful discharge, injuries to third parties and other claims.
- To ensure that the tax authorities also view independent contractors as indeed independent and not employees, the operator should have a written agreement with the contractor that specifies the nature and duration of the work to be done.

Practice Quiz

TRUE OR FALSE
On the following questions, answer whether the statement provided is true or false.

T   F   1. Under the law, all businesses are operated as proprietorships, partnerships, or corporations.

T   F   2. A partnership is legally defined under the Uniform Partnership Act as any venture where two or more persons endeavor to make a profit.

T   F   3. Double taxation occurs when the profits of a corporation are taxed and are then passed on to the owners, where the profits are again subject to taxation as individual income.

T   F   4. The owner of a restaurant never gets a depreciation allowance.

T   F   5. As sole proprietor, the restaurant operator draws a salary only for federal income tax purposes.

T   F   6. Depreciation, for tax purposes, bears a direct relationship to the actual decrease in the value of items being depreciated.

T   F   7. Anything that is a cost of doing business is tax deductible.

T   F   8. The owner of the land on which a restaurant sits gets a depreciation allowance.

T   F   9. A corporation is a legal entity similar to a person in that it can borrow, buy, conduct business, and must pay state and federal taxes on profits.

T   F   10. The simplest business entity, for tax purposes, is the sole proprietorship.

KEY TERM FILL IN THE BLANKS

On the following questions, fill in the blank with the most appropriate key term.

1. The _____ established a broad range of standards with respect to vesting, funding, and planned participation in pension plans.

2. Money set aside for replacing items that eventually have no value or only a salvage value is called a _____ allowance.

3. Medical expense reimbursement, sick pay, pension and profit-sharing plans are all examples of _____.

4. The _____ was designed to increase wages and increase employment by reducing the hours of the average workweek.

5. The _____ prohibits discrimination against persons who are disabled and stipulates that "readily achievable" modifications be made in work practices and working conditions, including physical access.

6. The _____ prohibits arbitrary discrimination of an employee based on their age, by private employers of 20 or more persons.

7. _____ have one or several co-owners, with only a general partner or partners making decisions, who are legally responsible if things go wrong.

8. The _____ bans discrimination based on race, religion, color, sex, and national origin.

9. Individual ownerships of a business are called _____.

10. Keogh and _____ plans can save a considerable amount of money for the individual. The total amount generated can be large because the interest generated is tax deferred and accumulates tax-free while the plans are in effect.

11. _____ partnerships share limited liability with no services performed.

12. The _____ is an amendment to the Fair Labor Standards Act, which prohibits employees from discriminating on the basis of sex by paying employees of one sex a lower rate than the opposite sex.

MULTIPLE CHOICE QUESTIONS: CONCEPT REVIEW

On the following questions, circle the choice that best answers the question.

1. There is a fee of about _____ for registering a new business with the state.
    a. $10
    b. $50
    c. $100
    d. $500

2. Keogh plans make it possible for a self-employed person or someone who has income from self-employment to put up to _____ per year or _____ percent of the annual income from the self-employment into a tax-sheltered retirement plan.
    a. $30,000; 33
    b. $20,000; 33
    c. $20,000; 25
    d. $30,000; 25

3. Which of the following is not tax deductible?
    a. company car
    b. life insurance
    c. low cost loans
    d. high cost loans

4. Workers' compensation insurance is:
    a. federally mandated but administered by the states.
    b. not federally mandated but administered by the states.
    c. federally mandated and administered.
    d. optional.

5. The law that was designed to increase wages and increase employment by reducing the hours of the average workweek is called the:
    a. Americans with Disabilities Act
    b. Fair Labor Standards Act
    c. Federal Equal Pay Act
    d. Age Discrimination in Employment Act

6. If the owners of a corporation do not want to accumulate after-tax income in the corporation, or if its shareholders are in low tax brackets or have personal tax loses, which of the following corporations is ideal?
    a. "P"
    b. "S"
    c. "L"
    d. "LL"

7. To ensure that the tax authorities also view independent contractors as indeed independent and not employees, the operator:
   a. should have a written agreement with the contractor that specifies the nature and duration of the work to be done.
   b. be in constant contact with the contractor's boss.
   c. a and b.
   d. none of the above.

8. Which of the following bans discrimination based on race, religion, color, sex, and national origin?
   a. Fair Labor Standards Act
   b. Civil Rights Act
   c. Federal Equal Pay Act
   d. Age Discrimination in Employment Act

9. Which of the following prohibits arbitrary discrimination based on the ages mentioned by private employers of 20 or more persons?
   a. Americans with Disabilities Act
   b. Fair Labor Standards Act
   c. Federal Equal Pay Act
   d. Age Discrimination in Employment Act

10. When incorporating, the first step should always be to:
    a. seek out a location.
    b. look for a partner.
    c. consult an attorney
    d. find financing.

11. Which can be depreciated for tax purposes over its expected life?
    a. food cost
    b. labor cost
    c. the building
    d. rent expenses

12. Which of the following established a broad range of standards with respect to vesting, funding, and planned participation in pension plans?
    a. Americans with Disabilities Act
    b. Fair Labor Standards Act
    c. Federal Equal Pay Act
    d. Employment Retirement Income Security Act

13. The DOL or state labor department officials may demand that a restaurant operator produce wage and hour records within:
   a. 24 hours.
   b. 50 hours.
   c. 60 hours.
   d. 72 hours.

14. Which of the following prohibits employers from discriminating based on sex by paying employees of one sex a lower rate than the opposite sex?
   a. Americans with Disabilities Act
   b. Fair Labor Standards Act
   c. Federal Equal Pay Act
   d. Age Discrimination in Employment Act

15. The simplest business entity, for tax purposes is the:
   a. sole proprietorship.
   b. limited liability corporation.
   c. partnerships.
   d. corporation.

SHORT ANSWER QUESTIONS

1. What benefits does workers' compensation insurance provide and how is it paid for? _____

_____

_____

_____

2. What is the National Labor Relations Act? _____

_____

_____

_____

3. Under federal law, what is the minimum permissible work age and what law mandates this?

_____

4. What time is not included in "hours worked"? _____

_____

_____

_____

CHAPTER 7: THE MENU

OBJECTIVES

- Identify factors to consider when planning a menu.

- List and describe some common menu types.

- Discuss methods for determining menu item pricing.

- Identify factors to consider when determining a menu's design and layout.

CHAPTER OUTLINE

The Menu
- The most important part of the restaurant concept.
- Requires careful analysis.
- Menu must reflect the concept and vice versa.
- Responsibility for developing the menu may begin with the chef, individually or in collaboration with the owner/manager and perhaps cooks and servers.

Capability/Consistency
- The capability of the chefs or cooks to produce the quality and quantity of food necessary is a basic consideration.
- Standardized recipes
  - List quantities of ingredients and step-by-step methods to produce a quality product.
- Elements that have an effect on capability and consistency:
  - Menu complexity.
  - Number of meals served.
  - Number of people to supervise.

Equipment
- Purchase the right equipment to achieve maximum production efficiency.
  - Many establishments plan the equipment according to the menu.
- Efficient layout:
  - Systematic flow of items from receiving clerk to guests assures operational efficiency.
- Avoid over use:
  - Too many menu items requiring one piece of equipment may slow service.

Availability
- Constant, reliable source of supply must be established.

- Must take advantage of seasonal items when they are at their lowest price and best quality.
- High-quality ingredients make a high quality product, and fresh must be that—Fresh!

Pricing

Factors in building price-value:
- Amount of product.
- Quality of product.
- Reliability or consistency of product.
- Uniqueness of product.
- Product options or choices.
- Service convenience.
- Comfort level.
- Reliability or consistency of service.
- Tie-in offers or freebies.

Pricing Strategies:

Two main ways to price a menu:
- Comparative approach
- Ratio method

Nutritional Value
- Greater public awareness of healthy food and individual wellness has prompted a change in cooking methods.
- Demand for healthier items like chicken and fish is increasing.
- Changes in type of cooking oil.
- Boiling, poaching, steaming, roasting, etc., as opposed to frying.
- Lower-fat menu items.
- More meatless and vegetarian options.

Contribution Margin
- Difference between the sales and the cost of the item.
- Amount goes toward covering fixed and variable costs.

Flavor
- Flavor is the sensory impression of a food or other substance determined by chemical senses.
- Taste involves all the senses:
    - Aroma
    - Texture
    - Sight
    - Sound

Accuracy
- Restaurants must be accurate and truthful when describing dishes on the menu.
- Some restaurants have been heavily fined for violations of accuracy in menu.

Kids' Menus
- Restaurants that cater to families usually have a separate kids' menu—one using bold colors and catchy make-believe characters.
- Most restaurants can provide fun placemats, crayons and small take-home prizes for kids.

Menu

Items:
- Independent restaurants tend to be more creative than chain restaurants.
- Menu items selected depend on type of restaurant.
- Appetizers and soups:
    - 6-8 is adequate for most establishments.
- Salads:
    - Preferred starter in many restaurants.
- Entrees:
    - At least 8 in a table-service restaurant.
- Desserts:
    - Can be purchased, made or finished off in-house.
- Matching/pairing:
    - Couple a type of wine with a general class of food.

Types:
- Dinner-house
- A la carte
- Table d'hôte
- Du jour menu
- Cyclical
- Menus are repeated in cycle every few days.
- California
- Tourist
- Degustation

Analysis:
- Should be a balance between a menu too high in food cost and too low in food cost.
- Menu engineering
    - Best menu items are those with highest contribution margin per unit and highest sales.
- It is recommended to analyze by:
    - Individual menu items.
    - Categories of menu offering.
    - Meal periods or business categories.

Design and Layout:
- Menu size may range from one to several pages.

- Come in a variety of shapes.
- Generally 9 × 12" or 11 × 17".
- Printing and artwork should harmonize with theme of the restaurant.
- The names of the dishes should be easy to read and understand.
- It should include a strong focal point.

Practice Quiz

TRUE OR FALSE
On the following questions, answer whether the statement provided is true or false.

T   F   1.   If the costs plus a profit cannot be covered, the restaurant should not be in operation and, over time, will fail.

T   F   2.   The cost of food varies with sales, a controllable expense.

T   F   3.   Federal law stipulates that businesses (including restaurants) may not misrepresent what they are selling.

T   F   4.   Vegan restaurants do not serve food heated above 116°F (46.7°C).

T   F   5.   Dinner-house menus separate similar entrées: beef in one section, seafood in another.

T   F   6.   The menu is the most important part of the restaurant concept.

T   F   7.   A table d'hôte menu offers a selection of several dishes from which patrons choose to make a complete meal at a fixed price.

T   F   8.   Four to five appetizers are adequate for the majority of restaurants.

T   F   9.   Operators use food and labor costs as a combination known as *prime cost,* which should be close to 55 to 60 and of sales.

T   F   10. The standardized recipe lists the quantities of ingredients and features a simple step-by-step method to produce a quality product.

FILL IN THE BLANKS: KEY TERM REVIEW
On the following questions, fill in the blank with the most appropriate key term.

1.   The use of standardized recipes and cooking procedures will help ensure the _____ of menu items.

2. The customer perception of the _____ value relationship and its comparison with competing restaurants is important.

3. Restaurant guests, some more than others, are becoming increasingly concerned about the _____ of food.

4. _____restaurants, such as Radha located in Manhattan, do not serve meat.

5. A constant, reliable source of supply at a reasonable price must be established and maintained and the menu items should be readily _____.

6. _____ is the sensory impression of a food or other substance determined chemical senses.

7. _____ is not heated above 116°F (46.7°C).

8. _____ means that if the trout on the menu comes from an Idaho trout farm, it cannot be described as coming from a more exotic-sounding location.

9. A _____ menu is a sample of the chef's best dishes.

10. The _____ is the difference between the sales price and the cost of the item.

11. The _____ of the chefs or cooks to produce the quality and quantity of food necessary is a basic consideration.

12. _____ have been called the silent salespersons of the restaurant. Overall, it should reflect the ambiance of the restaurant.

13. _____ restaurants exclude everything a vegetarian restaurant excludes, in addition to the exclusion of all dairy products.

14. The cost of ingredients must equal the predetermined_____.

15. In order to produce the desired menu items, the proper _____ must be installed in an efficient layout.

MULTIPLE CHOICE QUESTIONS: CONCEPT REVIEW
On the following questions, circle the choice that best answers the question.

1. Which of the following is the **most** important ingredient in providing guests with a pleasurable dining experience?
   a. management

b. hostess

c. location

d. menu

2. Which of the following will help ensure consistency for the restaurant?

a. use of standardized recipes

b. cooking procedures

c. location

d. a and b

3. There are two basic components of value creation:

a. what you provide and what you charge for it.

b. what you make for profits and what you charge for a product.

c. what you guests want to pay for an item and what you charge for it.

d. none of the above.

4. There are two main menu pricing strategies a:

a. relative approach and a comparative approach

b. individual menu item approach and value perception approach.

c. comparative approach and value perception approach.

d. comparative approach and the individual menu item approach.

5. A comparative approach analyzes:

a. the competition's prices and determines specials.

b. the individual menu items and multiplies them by the ratio amount necessary to achieve the required food cost percentage.

c. the competition's prices and determines the menu.

d. all the above.

6. Prime costs of a restaurant should be close to:

a. 30 to 35 percent of sales.

b. 40 to 45 percent of sales.

c. 55 to 60 percent of sales.

d. 65 to 70 percent of sales.

7. Raw bars or restaurants do not serve food:

a. above 75°F

b. below 75°F

c. above 116°F

d. below 116°F

8. The difference between the sales price and the cost of the item is called the:

a. ratio of expenditure.

b. contribution margin.

c. overhead expenses.

d. disbursement margin.

9. Which of the following is the sensory impression of a food or other substance determined chemical senses?
   a. taste
   b. smell
   c. texture
   d. all the above

10. With grilled salmon, nowadays, the wine of choice seems to be a:
    a. pinot noir.
    b. merlot.
    c. chardonnay.
    d. riesling.

11. Vegetarian restaurants:
    a. do not serve dairy.
    b. do not serve meat.
    c. serve chicken.
    d. b and c

12. Operators use food and labor costs as a combination known as:
    a. negligible costs.
    b. gross costs.
    c. real costs.
    d. prime costs.

13. The cost of ingredients must equal the:
    a. perception of value.
    b. predetermined food cost percentage.
    c. most profits.
    d. vacillating food cost percentage.

14. According to the text, the better of the two pricing strategies is the:
    a. relative approach.
    b. the individual menu item approach.
    c. comparative approach.
    d. value approach.

15. The standardized recipe lists:
    a. quantities of ingredients.
    b. a simple step-by-step method.
    c. a complex in depth method.
    d. a and b

SHORT ANSWER QUESTIONS

1.   What is a standardized recipe? _____

_____

_____

_____

2. Name 5 factors in building price-value? _____

_____

_____

_____

3. What is the contribution margin? _____

_____

_____

4. Name 4 types of menus. _____

_____

_____

_____

CHAPTER 8: PLANNING AND EQUIPPING THE KITCHEN

OBJECTIVES

- Identify factors to consider when planning a kitchen's layout.

- Discuss the benefits and drawbacks of an open kitchen.

- Explain selection factors for purchasing kitchen equipment.

- Identify various cooking techniques.

CHAPTER OUTLINE

Kitchen Planning
- The Overall Objective:
  - Minimize the number of steps taken by wait staff and kitchen personnel.
  - Equipment is placed so that servers only need to take a few steps.

The Open Kitchen
- Highlights the kitchen and/or a piece of equipment.
- Standard food preparation is not usually featured.
- The open kitchen is reserved for what is glamorous: bright, shiny ladles, stainless steel and copper utensils, etc.
- Some use under the counter refrigerator units to conserve space.
- The area set aside for open kitchens costs about 25% more than a standard kitchen.
Drawbacks:
  - The noise level of a completely open kitchen must be reduced with washable acoustic tile in the ceiling.
  - The dining room and banquet rooms must feature carpet, upholstered chairs, washable window drapes, and acoustic ceilings (to absorb kitchen noise).
  - Chefs and cooks are completely exposed to the customers:
    - Every word and every gesture has a spectator.
  - Customers may also feel that since they can see the chefs and/or cooks that it is okay to talk to them.

Kitchen Floor Coverings
- Materials should be nonabsorbent, easy to clean and resistant to the abrasive action of cleaners.
  - Kitchen floors are usually covered with quarry tile, marble, terrazzo, asphalt tile, or sealed concrete.
- In areas that accumulate water, neoprene matting provides traction.
- All kitchen areas should be covered with nonskid materials.
- The number-one cause of restaurant accidents is slipping and falling.

Kitchen Equipment Categories
- Receiving and storing food
- Fabricating and preparing food
- Preparing and processing food
- Assembling, holding, and serving food
- Cleaning up/sanitizing the kitchen and kitchenware

Menu Determines Kitchen Equipment
- Variables include the following:
    - The projected volume of sales for each menu item.
    - Fixed or changing menu.
    - Menu size.
    - Speed of service desired.
    - Nutritional awareness and equipment selected.

Cooking Equipment:
- The Oven/Stove
- Deep-Frying Equipment
- Low Temperature Ovens
- Forced-Air Convection Ovens
- Microwave Ovens
- Infrared Cooking Equipment
- Hot-Food Holding Tables
- Refrigerators and Freezers
- Ice machines
- Pasta-Making Machines
- Evaporative Coolers
- Numerous other kitchen items are available that may be useful for a particular menu:
    - Ice cream holding units, display cases, cream dispensers, meat patty–making machines, garbage disposals, infrared heating lamps, drink dispensers, dough dividers, bakers' stoves, etc.

Meeting with the Health Inspector
- Public health officials and planning boards want to assure the public that eating in restaurants under their jurisdiction is safe.
- To this end, local health officers draw up extensive requirements for a number of factors, including:
    - Floor covering
    - No. of toilets
    - Foodservice equipment
    - Lighting
    - Fire exits
- Requirements vary from place to place.

- Floor drainage systems, exhaust ductwork, distances between dining room tables, # of seats permitted, # of parking spaces required, # of entrances and exits to the parking area and to the restaurant—all must meet safety requirements.

Practice Quiz

TRUE OR FALSE
On the following questions, answer whether the statement provided is true or false.

T   F   1.   The microwave oven has high value for producing baked-dough items and any type of food that involves a leavening action.

T   F   2.   Kitchen floors are usually covered with quarry tile, marble, terrazzo, asphalt tile, or sealed concrete.

T   F   3.   Ergonomics is the applied science of equipment design intended to reduce staff fatigue and discomfort.

T   F   4.   In a full-service restaurant, stovetops, ovens, and broilers are the dominate pieces of kitchen equipment.

T   F   5.   Open kitchens are decreasing in popularity due to various disadvantages.

T   F   6.   The microwave oven should never be used in a restaurant kitchen.

T   F   7.   Carpeting in kitchens is permitted by building codes but not advisable.

T   F   8.   The number-one cause of restaurant accidents is slipping and falling.

T   F   9.   The area set aside for open kitchens costs about 10% more than a standard kitchen.

T   F   10. An overall objective of layout planning is to minimize the number of steps taken by wait staff and kitchen personnel.

FILL IN THE BLANKS: KEY TERM REVIEW
On the following questions, fill in the blank with the most appropriate key term.

1.   A _____ or _____ can be thought of as two boxes, one inside the other, separated by insulation.

2.   Food is prepared and rapidly chilled to prevent bacterial growth and is available in portions of various sizes. This is called the _____ method.

3. The _____ is now being used by several fast-food hamburger chains. The employee only needs to place frozen patties of hamburger on the conveyor belt, which carries the patties through flames directed from above and below.

4. _____ with ovens is often done during the night, which frees up oven space for daytime use.

5. _____, which permit low-temperature roasting and baking, are widely used in the restaurant business to reduce shrinkage of meat and to hold meat so that it can be served to order from the oven.

6. Probably the most prominent piece of equipment in the full-service kitchen is the _____, the combination stove and oven, fired by gas or electricity.

7. The standard equipment needed in restaurant kitchens can be divided according to purpose or into _____.

8. The _____ technique is when food is prepared, individually vacuum packed and refrigerated for future use.

9. Operators use _____ to boil seafood, vegetables, and pasta products.

10. A _____ is similar to a conventional oven except that a fan or rotor, usually located in the back, makes for rapid circulation of the air, which results in quicker heating of the food.

MULTIPLE CHOICE QUESTIONS: CONCEPT REVIEW
On the following questions, circle the choice that best answers the question.

1. The area set aside for open kitchens costs about _____ percent more than in a standard kitchen.
   a. 10
   b. 15
   c. 20
   d. 25

2. Which of the following pieces of kitchen equipment permits low-temperature roasting and baking?
   a. hot food holding tables
   b. microwaves
   c. low-temperature ovens
   d. forced-air convection oven

3. Because microwaves are absorbed preferentially by water:
   a. they should never be used in restaurants.
   b. cooking is not uniform.

c. a and b.
d. none of the above.

4.   Food is prepared and rapidly chilled to prevent bacterial growth and is available in portions of various sizes during the:
a. sous-vide method.
b. cook-chill process.
c. sous-chill process.
d. a and b.

5.   Evaporative coolers installed in kitchens:
a. reduce the cost of cooling considerably where humidity in the outside air is low.
b. reduce the cost of cooling considerably where humidity in the outside air is high.
c. overall increase the cost of cooling.
d. are never recommended.

6.   Restaurant equipment is generally thought to have a life expectancy of about:
a. 1 year.
b. 3 years.
c. 7 years.
d. 10 years.

7.   Infrared wavelengths used for cooking are only microns in length. Wavelengths of about ___ to ___ microns are said to be the most effective for cooking foods.
a. 0 to 1
b. 1.4 to 5
c. 5 to 6.14
d. 7 to 10.14

8.   According to the text, after being purchased restaurant equipment may drop as much as ___ percent in value.
a. 80
b. 85
c. 90
d. 95

9.   The menu determines the:
a. staff.
b. equipment.
c. location.
d. none of the above.

10. McDonald's restaurants are built around a:
a. griddle.
b. convection oven.
c. deep fryer.

d. a and c.

11. Food is individually vacuum packed and refrigerated for future use during the:
    a. sous vide method.
    b. cook-chill process.
    c. sous-chill process.
    d. a and b.

12. In a Chinese restaurant, the equipment star is the:
    a. griddle.
    b. convection oven.
    c. deep fryer.
    d. wok.

13. As additional items are placed in the oven, heating or cooking time may increase by ___ percent or more per item.
    a. 25
    b. 50
    c. 75
    d. 90

14. Probably the most prominent piece of equipment in the full-service kitchen is the:
    a. convection oven.
    b. tilting skillet.
    c. range.
    d. microwave.

15. Because evaporative coolers have no need of compressors, they operate at approximately ___ percent of the cost of operating a refrigerated air-conditioning unit of similar cooling capacity.
    a. 10
    b. 15
    c. 20
    d. 25

SHORT ANSWER QUESTIONS

1. What is the overall goal of kitchen planning? _____

_____

_____

_____

2. Name 3 kitchen equipment categories. _____

_____

_____

_____

3. What is the goal of a health inspection? _____

_____

_____

_____

CHAPTER 9: FOOD PURCHASING

OBJECTIVES

- Explain the importance of product specifications.

- List and describe the steps for creating a purchasing system.

- Identify factors to consider when establishing par stocks and reordering points.

- Explain selection factors for purchasing meat, produce, canned goods, coffee and other items.

CHAPTER OUTLINE

Food Specifications
- Written standards for food (food specifications) are set before a restaurant opens.
- The amounts to purchase are based on a forecast of sales.
- When in operation, par stocks (the reasonable amount to have on hand) and reorder points (the stock points that indicate more should be ordered) are established.

Steps in a Food Purchasing System
- Determine the quality of food standards required to serve the market.
- Develop product specifications.
- Gather product-availability information.
- Have alternate suppliers in mind.
- Select a person to order and receive supplies.

Steps in a Purchasing System
- Set up storage space for maximum utilization.
- Establish the amount needed to be stocked- par stock – each item.
- Set up inventory system.
- Decide on optimal delivery size to reduce cost of delivery and handling.
- Check all inventories for quality and quantity/weight.
- Tie inventory control and cost control system together.

The Purchasing Cycle
- A purchasing cycle can be set up that rolls along efficiently, a system that repeats itself day after day with minimal demands on the operator.
- Product specifications need only be reviewed not reset, each time food is ordered.
- Par stock and reorder points are relatively fixed and changed only as sales volume changes appreciably or as the menu changes.
- Major suppliers are changed infrequently.

Food Quality Standards
- Standards for food quality are set to serve a particular market:
    - Some operators serve fresh fish only, never frozen.
    - Some restaurants use only fresh vegetables.

Buying by Specification
- Each operation needs a quality of food that fits its market.
- The quality needed varies with the market and also with the food item being produced.
    - Canned vegetables used in a made-up dish need not be of fancy grade.
    - Meat for grinding into hamburger may well come from U.S. good or even lower-graded meat and still be satisfactory.

Par Stocks and Reorder Points
- Based on quantity used, storage space available and availability of the product.
- Fast moving items require more stock.
- The operator with a fixed menu has an advantage in buying.

Types of Purchasing
- <u>Full-line purveyors</u>:
    - Carry a large line of supplies
    - Offer more one stop shopping
    - Saves time
    - Simplified billing
- <u>Co-op Buying</u>
    - Supplies products at cost, plus enough of a markup to cover the cooperative's cost.
    - Nonprofit
    - Lower cost than profit

USDA Wholesale Produce Grades
- U.S. Fancy: Applies to highly specialized produce- Rarely used.
- U.S. No. 1: Most widely used in trading produce from farm to market.
- U.S. Commercial: This grade applies to produce inferior to U.S. No. 1 but superior to U.S. No. 2.
- U.S. Combination: Combines percentages of U.S. No. 1 and U.S. No. 2.
- U.S. No. 2: Usually considered the lowest quality practical to ship- Poorer appearance and more waste than U.S. No. 1.
- U.S. No. 3: Produce used for highly specialized products.

Practice Quiz

TRUE OR FALSE
On the following questions, answer whether the statement provided is true or false.

T   F   1. With a new process called *flash freezing,* fish are immersed in a liquid chemical that brings them to 100 degrees Fahrenheit.

T   F   2. Product specifications need only be reviewed, not reset, each time food is ordered.

T   F   3. Restaurateurs are letting the menu drive business, and many change menus and prices four times a year.

T   F   4. Nearly every food that contains a large amount of water expands with storage.

T   F   5. A co-op is a nonprofit institution that is able to provide restaurant food and supplies at lower cost than the profit-oriented purveyors.

T   F   6. Par stock and reorder points are relatively fixed and are changed only as sales volume changes appreciably or as the menu changes.

T   F   7. U.S. Fancy grade is the most widely used grade in trading produce from farm to market and indicates good/average quality.

T   F   8. In independent restaurants, the responsibility for food purchasing usually rests with the cook.

T   F   9. Quality standards and standard fill of container are concerns of the FDA.

T   F 10. When it comes to the par stock for canned foods, the amount that is considered a safe inventory may be ordered only when the supply is down to a specified amount.

FILL IN THE BLANKS: KEY TERM REVIEW
On the following questions, fill in the blank with the most appropriate key term.

1. The reasonable amount of a product to have on hand is called _____.

2. A _____ calls for a par stock and a reorder point for each food item.

3. Written standards for food called _____ are set, preferably in writing, before a restaurant opens.

4. The *U.S.* _____ grade applies to produce that combines percentages of U.S. No. 1 and U.S. No. 2.

5   _____ can be thought of as a subsystem within the total restaurant system, which once installed can be set in motion, and can repeat itself.

6.   The *U.S.* _____ grade is the most widely used grade in trading produce from farm to market and indicates good/average quality.

7.   The U.S. _____ grade applies to highly specialized produce, a very small percentage of the total crop and is rarely used on most commodities because it is too costly to pack.

8.   The U.S. _____ grade applies to produce used for highly specialized products.

9.   The stock points that indicate more product should be ordered are called_____.

10.   _____ control—the amount of food to be ordered and stocked—can be built into the purchasing system by reference to past records.

MULTIPLE CHOICE QUESTIONS: CONCEPT REVIEW
On the following questions, circle the choice that best answers the question.

1.   The system that uses the price actually paid for the item is called:
      a. LIFO
      b. FIFO
      c. LILO
      d. PIPO

2.   Restaurants with lower-priced menus are likely to:
      a. feature fruits that are out of season.
      b. feature fruits that are in season.
      c. feature more vegetables than fruits.
      d. features a lot of meat.

3.   Who is responsible for maintaining inspection services at principal shipping points and terminal markets?
      a. customs
      b. the shipper
      c. the USDA
      d. the receivers

4.   The lowest grade of produce quality practical to ship is:
      a. U.S. No. 1
      b. U.S. No. 2
      c. U.S. No. 3

d. U.S. No. 4

5. Standards and the standard fill of can containers are concerns of the:
    a. USDA
    b. MBA
    c. FDA
    d. none of the above

6. Par stock and reorder point of each food item in the purchasing system is based on _____.
    a. quantities used
    b. storage space availability
    c. availability of product
    d. all of the above

7. The grade of meat that is the most widely used grade in trading produce from farm to market and indicates good/average quality is known as:
    a. U.S. No. 1
    b. U.S. No. 2
    c. U.S. No. 3
    d. U.S. No. 4

8. Operators who frequently use canned fruits or vegetables perform can-cutting tests, usually in the:
    a. fall.
    b. spring.
    c. summer.
    d. winter.

9. The best way to select coffee is to:
    a. inspect the beans for oil.
    b. consult a coffee expert.
    c. taste it yourself.
    d. serve it to a taste panel of typical patrons.

10. With a new process called flash freezing:
    a. fish are immersed in a liquid chemical that gets them to 265 degrees.
    b. fish is frozen so fast that water molecules do not crystallize.
    c. fish is vacuum packed.
    d. a and b.

11. Food storage in a restaurant is arranged purposely to facilitate _____.
    a. receiving
    b. issuing
    c. inventory control
    d. all of the above

12. A "can cutting" test should determine _____.
    a. the net drained weight
    b. the strength of the container
    c. the viscosity of the liquid
    d. none of the above

13. A system which costs the item at the price paid for the merchandise purchased last is _____.
    a. LIFO
    b. FIFO
    c. LILO
    d. PIPO

14. Par stocks are:
    a. the reasonable amount of items to have on hand.
    b. stock points that indicate more items should be ordered.
    c. none of the above.
    d. a and b.

15. The length of time an item can be stored without appreciable loss in quality or weight is called _____.
    a. maintenance period
    b. freshness time
    c. shelf life
    d. safety period

SHORT ANSWER QUESTIONS

1. What are the 5 steps in a food purchasing system? _____

_____

_____

_____

_____

2. What are the 6 steps in a purchasing cycle? _____

_____

_____

_____

_____

_____

3. What do full line purveyors provide? _____

_____

_____

_____

4. What are the characteristics of co-op buying? _____

_____

_____

_____

5. What is the purpose of following buying specification? _____

_____

_____

_____

CHAPTER 10: FOOD PRODUCTION AND SANITATION

OBJECTIVES

- Discuss America's culinary heritage
- Explain the main elements in receiving and storing perishable and non-perishable items.
- Describe the key points in food production
- Discuss the various types of food poisoning and how to avoid them
- Develop and maintain a food protection system

CHAPTER OUTLINE

Our Culinary Heritage
- American cooking was formed on a matrix of national cuisines, the confluence of foods and food preparation methods from numerous national and racial groups.
    - English, Italian, Indian, French, Chinese, etc.

The Italian Influence
- Italian food has a rich tradition and offers a variety of foods.
- Italians cultivated fine cuisine long before the French.
- In the ancient period, the wealthy Romans spent lavishly in time and money on food and drink.

The French Influence
- When it comes to classic culinary terms, the vast majority are straight from the kitchens of France.
    - Blanch, fricassee, poach, almandine, etc.
- Most foodservice experts rank French cookery near or at the top of various national cuisines.

French Chefs Dominate Culinary History
- Vatel (maitre d'hotel to the Prince de Conde)
- Francois Pierre de La Varenne
- Antonine Careme
- Felix Urbain-DuBois
- Georges August Escoffier
- Monseiur Boulanger

French Sauces
- Sauces, particularly those thickened with roux (equal quantities of fat and flour) were the hallmarks of the French cook.

- There are five "mother" or leading sauces:
  - Béchamel (or White Sauce): Usually made today by whisking scalded milk gradually into a white flour-butter roux. In the original French version, Béchamel was made with veal stock.
  - Veloute: A light stock, such as chicken, veal or fish stock, is thickened with a blond roux.
  - Espagnole (or Brown Sauce): Typically prepared from vegetables and herbs that are cooked in a brown roux, to which a dark stock (veal or beef) and tomato purée are then added.
  - Hollandaise: An emulsion of butter and lemon juice using egg yolks as the emulsifying agent, usually seasoned with salt and a little black pepper or cayenne pepper.
  - Tomato: Any of a very large number of sauces made primarily out of tomatoes.

- Younger French chefs have invented ways of avoiding calories while retaining flavor.
- Fresh foods, lower fat, and the avoidance of roux-thickened sauces are being featured.
  - These are called Nouvelle Cuisine (The New Cuisine) and Cuisine Minceur (pronounced man sir) the "cuisine of thinness".
    - Instead of roux-thickened sauces, pureed fruits and vegetables are used and liquids are reduced by cooking to appropriate thickness.

Receiving
- Smart restaurateurs arrange with suppliers for all deliveries to be delivered at times continent to the restaurant.
- It is critically important that a copy of the order be available for the receiver and to check that the quality and quantity was accurate per the order.
- Management should check and sign for all deliveries.

Storage
- Storage should be arranged for easy receiving, easy issuing and easy inventory control.
- In the dry-goods storeroom, canned, packed, and bulk dry foods are stored according to usage.
  - The most-used foods are stored closest to the door, the least-used foods in the less accessible corners and shelves.
- In costing an inventory, the last-in, first-out (LIFO) system costs the item at the price paid for the merchandise purchased last.
- The first-in, first-out (FIFO) system uses the price actually paid for the item.

Food Production
- The kitchen manager, chef or cook begins the production process by determining the expected number of guests for the next few days.
  - The same period for the previous year can give a good indication of the expected volume and breakdown of the number of sales of each menu item.
  - The product mix (a list of what was sold yesterday) will give an indication of what needs to be 'prepped' in order to bring the item back up to its 'par' level.

- Every morning the chef or kitchen manager determines the amount of each menu item to prepare.
- The par levels of those menu items in the refrigerators are checked and a production sheet is completed for each station in the kitchen.
- The cooking line is the most important part of the kitchen layout.
  - It might consist of a broiler station, window station, fry station, salad station, sauté station and dessert station.
- The kitchen is set up according to what the guests order more frequently.

Production Procedures
- Production in the kitchen is critical to the success of a restaurant since it relates directly to the recipes on the menu and how much product is on hand to produce the menu.
  - Timing is also crucial.
- Production starts with **mise-en-place** (the assembly of ingredients and equipment for the recipe) because the backbone for every service in the restaurant is the ingredients being 'prepped' for all the recipes.
- The first step in creating the production sheets is to count the products on hand for each station.
- Once the production levels are determined, the amount of production required to reach the level for each recipe is decided.
- When these calculations are completed, the sheets are handed to the cooks.
- The use of production sheets is critical, in controlling how the cooks use the products since production plays a key role in food cost.
- Every recipe has a particular "spec" (specification) to follow.
- When one deviates from the recipe, the quality goes down, consistency is lost, and food cost goes up.
- When determining production, par levels should be changed according to sales trends.
  - This will help control and minimize waste levels.
  - Waste is a large contributor to food cost.

Staffing and Scheduling
- Practicing proper staffing is absolutely critical for the successful running of a kitchen.
- It is important to have enough staff on the schedule to enable the restaurant to handle the volume on any shift.
- Often it is better to overstaff the kitchen, rather than under-staff it, for two reasons.
  - First, it is much easier to send an employee home than it is to call someone in.
  - Second, having extra staff on hand allows for cross-training and development, which is becoming a widely used method.

Food Borne Illness
- The United States Public Health Service identifies more than 40 diseases that can be transferred through food.
- Many can cause serious illness; some are even deadly.
- A food-borne illness is a disease that is carried or transmitted to human beings by food.
- There are three types of hazards to safe food: biological, chemical, and physical.

- Of these three, biological hazards cause the highest percentage of food-borne illness outbreaks.

Biological Hazards-Bacteria
- The highest number of biological food-borne illness is caused by bacteria, single-celled microorganisms that are capable of reproducing in about 20 minutes.
- Bacteria, like all living organisms, need sustenance to function and multiply.
- Bacteria can cause illness in two ways:
  - The first is via disease-causing bacteria, known as *pathogens,* which feed on nutrients in hazardous foods and given favorable conditions, multiply rapidly.
  - Other bacteria, while not being harmful themselves, do, as they multiply, discharge toxins that poison humans when food containing them is eaten.
- Pathogenic bacteria can cause illness in humans in one of the three ways:
  - Intoxication.
  - Infection.
  - Toxin-mediated infection.

Causes of Food Borne Illness
- High protein foods that we eat regularly are responsible for most food-borne illnesses.
  - These include any food that *consists in* whole or *in* part of milk or milk products, shell eggs, meats, poultry, fish, shellfish, edible crustacea (shrimp, lobster, crab, etc.) baked or boiled potatoes, tofu and other soy-protein foods, plant foods that have been heat treated, raw seed sprouts, or synthetic ingredients.
- The three disease-causing microorganisms most commonly associated with food borne illness in the United States are:
  - Staphylococcus aureus.
  - Salmonella.
  - Clostridium perfringem.

Controlling or Destroying Bacteria
- In order to grow, bacteria require food, moisture, the proper pH, and time.
- Among the potentially hazardous foods are those high in protein, like meat, milk and dairy products, especially eggs, fish, and shellfish.
- Items like custard, mayonnaise, hollandaise sauce, and quiche are particularly susceptible to contamination.

Bacteria and Temperature
- Temperature is the most important element for bacteria survival and growth; it is also the easiest for restaurateurs to control.
  - The temperature danger zone—between 40°F and 140°F—is the range in which bacteria can thrive and multiply most rapidly.
- Most bacteria, harmful or not, are destroyed by heat.
- Three commonly used chemical sanitizers are chlorine, quaternary compounds, and iodine.
- Dishes and utensils are immersed for one minute in solution at least 75°F in temperature.

Viruses

- Viruses do not require a hazardous food in order to survive.
  - They can survive on any food or surface, do not multiply, and are not as affected by heat or cold, as are bacteria.
  - They simply use the food or other surface as means of transportation.
- Once the virus enters a body cell, it takes over, forcing the cell to assist in the production of more viruses.

Chemical Contaminants

- The increased use of pesticides has caused concern about the chemical contamination of foods.
- Besides pesticides, there are four types of chemical contamination that can occur at any point along the food supply chain:
  - Restaurant chemicals like detergents and sanitizers.
  - Preservatives and additives.
  - Acidic reaction of foods with metal-lined containers.
  - Contamination of food with toxic metals.

Hazard Analysis of Critical Control Points

1. Identify hazards and assess their severity and risks.
2. Determine critical control points (CCPs) in food preparation.
3. Determine critical control limits (CCLs) for each CCP identified.
4. Monitor CCPs and record data.
5. Take corrective action whenever monitoring indicates a CCL is exceeded.
6. Establish an effective record-keeping system to document the HACCP system.
7. Establish procedures to verify that the HACCP system is working.

Common Food Safety Mistakes

- Some of the most common food safety risks in day-to-day food production fall into three key areas:
  - Time/temperature abuse.
  - Cross-contamination.
  - Poor personal hygiene.

Food Protection as a System

- Up to a point, the more sanitation practices that can be built into a system, the more likely they will be carried out.
- Personnel trained in the system are carried along by it.
- One of the reasons for the success of chains like McDonald's is their emphasis on the sanitation system.
- To systematize sanitation practices, they should be built into the manager's daily schedule.

Practice Quiz

TRUE OR FALSE
On the following questions, answer whether the statement provided is true or false.

T   F   1.   Historically, the French cultivated fine cuisine long before the Italians.

T   F   2.   Cuisine Minceur is the "cuisine of thinness."

T   F   3.   French cuisine includes literally hundreds of sauces but basically, there are eight "mother" or leading sauces, each with a number of variations.

T   F   4.   Fusion cuisine is a blending of the techniques and ingredients of two different cuisines – such as Japanese and French.

T   F   5.   In costing an inventory, the LIFO system costs the item at the price paid for the merchandise purchased last.

T   F   6.   When it comes to classic culinary terms, the vast majority are straight from the kitchens of Italy.

T   F   7.   The cooking line is the most important part of the kitchen layout.

T   F   8.   Production starts with mise-en-place.

T   F   9.   The product mix is a list of what was sold on the same day last year.

T   F   10. The Escoffier Cookbook became the bible for thousands of cooks for many years.

FILL IN THE BLANKS: KEY TERM REVIEW
On the following questions, fill in the blank with the most appropriate key term.

1.   Traditional French cookery, especially that of _____, the complex, expensive cookery, was concerned with 'working over' foods, long cooking times, the making of forcemeats, shaping and turning vegetables, and combining foods in familiar ways.

2.   _____ in the kitchen is critical to the success of a restaurant since it relates directly to the recipes on the menu and how much product is on hand to produce the menu.

3.   The first is via disease-causing bacteria, known as_____, feed on nutrients in hazardous foods and, given favorable conditions, multiply rapidly.

4.   _____ is the blending of the techniques and ingredients of two different cuisines—such as Mediterranean and Chinese or Thai and Italian.

5. The _____ may consist of a broiler station, window station, fry station, salad station, sauté station and desert station—just to name a few.

6. _____ is the assembly of ingredients and equipment for the recipe.

7. The _____ gives the quantity of each menu item to be prepared and increases the efficiency and productivity by eliminating guesswork.

8. Every morning the chef or kitchen manager determines the amount of each menu item to prepare and then _____ of those menu items in the refrigerators are checked.

9. _____ chefs dominate culinary history.

10. In costing an inventory, _____ system costs the item at the price paid for the merchandise purchased last. The _____ system uses the price actually paid for the item.

MULTIPLE CHOICE QUESTIONS: CONCEPT REVIEW
On the following questions, circle the choice that best answers the question.

1. The temperature danger zone-between _____ and _____ is the range in which bacteria can thrive and multiply most rapidly.
   a. 20°F and 40°F
   b. 40°F and 140°F
   c. 120°F and 140°F
   d. 140°F and 160°F

2. Symptoms of staph. appear in:
   a. 1 to 2 hours.
   b. 2 to 6 hours.
   c. 6 to 12 hours.
   d. immediately.

3. High-protein foods are:
   a. as hazardous as other types of food.
   b. responsible for most of food borne illness.
   c. less hazardous than other types of food.
   d. b and c.

4. Peifringens symptoms appear:
   a. 1 to 2 hours after consumption.
   b. 8 to 24 hours after consumption.
   c. 24 to 36 hours after consumption.
   d. 36 to 52 fours after consumption.

5. Which of the following causes a majority of the tourist symptoms commonly experienced in developing nations?
   a. Salmonella
   b. Staph
   c. E.coli
   d. Ebola

6. Salmonella symptoms normally show up:
   a. 2 to 6 hours after eating.
   b. 1 to 3 hours after eating.
   c. 12 to 36 hours after eating.
   d. 42 to 56 hours after eating.

7. What chefs dominate culinary history?
   a. American
   b. Italian
   c. German
   d. French

8. Which of the following became the bible for thousands of cooks for many years?
   a. The Escoffier Cookbook
   b. The Joy of Cooking
   c. The Joy of Eating
   d. Moosewoods

9. Velvety smooth sauces made from either thickened veal, fish, or chicken stock are called:
   a. Veloute.
   b. Bechamel.
   c. Espagnole.
   d. Hollandaise.

10. Salmonella presents no problem if suspect foods are heated to:
    a. 125°F.
    b. 135°F.
    c. 145°F.
    d. 165°F.

11. Working over foods, long cooking times, and the making of forced meats are all characteristics of:
    a. haute cuisine.
    b. nouvelle cuisine.
    c. sous-vide cuisine
    d. all the above.

12. Salmonella symptoms normally last:
    a. a day or two.
    b. two days to a week.
    c. until treated.
    d. forever.

13. The blending of techniques and ingredients from different types of cuisine id known as:
    a. haute cuisine.
    b. nouvelle cuisine.
    c. sous-vide cuisine
    d. fusion cuisine.

14. Symptoms of staph. last:
    a. a day or two.
    b. a week.
    c. until treated.
    d. forever.

15. Restaurants should hold foods at internal temperatures of at least:
    a. 70°F.
    b. 90°F.
    c. 120°F.
    d. 140°F.

SHORT ANSWER QUESTIONS

1. What does *mise-en-place* mean and what does it have to do with production? _____

_____

_____

_____

2. What 3 areas are the most common food safety risks in day-to-day food production? _____

_____

_____

_____

3. Besides pesticides, what are the 4 types of chemical contamination that can occur at any point along the food supply chain? _____

_____

_____

_____

4. How do viruses survive and thrive? _____

_____

_____

_____

CHAPTER 11: SERVICE AND CUSTOMER RELATIONS

OBJECTIVES

- Describe characteristics of effective servers and greeters.

- Identify the seven commandments of customer service.

- List guidelines for handling customer complaints.

CHAPTER OUTLINE

The Service Encounter
- Many servers are skilled performers in the service encounter.
- The server and the guest are both actors in the play.
- Once the meal is finished, the play is over, the guest leaves and the server moves on to the next stage.

Gamesmanship
- Many servers look at the customer–server relationship as a battle of wits, with the guest as the opponent.
- The object of the game is to extract the maximum tip possible.
- At the end of each evening, word is passed as to who received the most in tips.
- If servers are pitted against each other and there are prizes for who gets the most tips, it is easy for a dining room to degenerate into a game, with the guest as secondary participant.
- One way to ensure harmony among all of the restaurant's personnel is to insist that all tips be pooled and everyone share.

What Makes a Good Server
- Personality.
- Team orientation.
- Technical knowledge of product/tableside confidence.
- Knowledge of how to read guests and anticipate their needs.
- Knowledge of the finer points of service.

Greeters
- The first and last person a guest encounters.
- A smiling, well-groomed, friendly person is an asset to the restaurant, but the position calls for more.
  - Greeters who know the restaurant add luster and are able to answer a variety of specific (and general) questions.
- The main part of the host/hostess's job is to represent the restaurant by offering a friendly greeting and facilitating the seating of guests.

- Another key aspect of the job is knowing how to seat guests and not overload a server or the kitchen.
- Greeters keep a sheet for reservations, whether they are called in or walk-ins.

Food Service Teams
- Some restaurants operate with servers working two to a team.
- Most common is the server/busser team.
- Some systems work as the entire crew makes up the team.
- "Full Hands In, Full Hands Out"—helps everyone work to help each other.
- The team system has one major advantage: Hot food is served hot.

Hard Sell Versus Soft Sell
- The hard sell: May result in the customer feeling pressured.
    - "Will you have dessert?"
    - "Would you like a cocktail?"
- The soft sell: Low-key complete service.
- The kind of clientele may determine the best approach.
- Service includes a number of factors other than selling including showmanship, wine service, attention to detail, refilling water glasses, cleaning ashtrays, replacing soiled silver, etc.

Seven Commandments of Customer Service
1. Tell the truth.
2. Bend the rules.
3. Listen actively.
4. Put pen to paper.
5. Master the moments of truth.
6. Be a fantastic fixer.
7. Never underestimate the value of a thank you.

Formality or Informality
- This depends on the kind of experience you are trying to deliver.
- Some restaurants thrive on informality.
- Others may be more formal and the servers only speak when spoken to.

The Difficult Guest
- Once in a while, the server is confronted by a difficult guest.
- The majority of complaint handling falls into the employee hands.
- Employees have to be trained to problem solve the right way and right away!
- The approach is, "What can I do to help?"
    - Which is, in itself, is quite disarming.

Win-Win Action Tips
- Act immediately on a complaint.
- Let the customer know you care.
- Calm the customer by acknowledging the problem and encouraging feedback.

- Tell the customer in an honest way how the problem will be addressed.
- Invite the customer to express his or her feelings.
- Never invalidate or make the customer wrong.
- Offer appropriate and reasonable amends.
- Nurture the relationship by smiling and thanking the customer again.

Strategies for Handling Complaints
- Remain calm.
- Listen.
- Empathize.
- Control your voice.
- Get the facts.
- Take care of the problem immediately.
- If you take back an entrée, offer to keep the meals of the other diners warm in the kitchen, so that the group can eat together.

Service Personnel as a Family
- Many managers do whatever they can to create a family feeling among foodservice personnel:
    - Encourage employees to eat and drink on the premises.
    - Reduce meal prices.
    - Sponsor employee parties.

Practice Quiz

TRUE OR FALSE
On the following questions, answer whether the statement provided is true or false.

T   F   1. Various kinds of dining room service organization exist, the server/busser combination being the most common.

T   F   2. When it comes to customer service, honesty is the best policy.

T   F   3. Restaurant literature and educational programs uniformly urge service personnel to promote and sell as part of the service job.

T   F   4. Ambiance is often ranked as the most important factor in restaurant selection by patrons oppose to service.

T   F   5. The majority of complaint handling falls into the employee hands.

T   F   6. Servers can expect fewer problems from people seated in open spaces.

T   F   7. Service quality is the least frequent complaint made by restaurant patrons.

T F 8. Once you know the reason for the rule and its boundaries, go ahead and bend it, if that is what it takes to make the system better serve your customer.

T F 9. The food order should be taken by asking the female to the right of you for her order first, followed by the other women.

T F 10. In many restaurants, servers are selected, in large part, based on appearance—the best-looking women and the handsomest men.

FILL IN THE BLANKS: KEY TERM REVIEW
On the following questions, fill in the blank with the most appropriate key term.

1. Many servers are skilled performers in the _____. The dinner house, and especially the lounge, is the stage.

2. Once in a while, the server is confronted by a _____ who is determined to prove his manhood or vent his hostility on other customers, the serving personnel, or the manager personally.

3. Service personnel must be aware of the degree of _____ desired by their customers.

4. Servers should get down to eye level and make _____ with their _____.

5. Servers must be willing to participate in a _____ effort. They have to be willing to contribute to the guest's satisfaction, whether or not they are in their section.

6. When low-key, complete service is expected, servers should go with a _____.

7. When tables are plentiful, the question could be, "Would you prefer a table or a booth?" This is an example of _____.

MULTIPLE CHOICE QUESTIONS: CONCEPT REVIEW
On the following questions, circle the choice that best answers the question.

1. Which of the following facilitates social interaction among those seated together in a restaurant?
    a. social distance from other patrons.
    b. walls visually blocking some stimuli.
    c. seating them in the center of the restaurant.
    d. a and b

2. If the individual is noticeably shy or ill at ease and comes into a restaurant alone, they should be seated:
    a. at a bar table.
    b. in the center of the restaurant.
    c. in a booth.
    d. with another group of patrons.

3. In some establishments, everyone shares tips on a fixed-ratio basis (including the kitchen), a practice common in Europe and the Middle East; this is called the:
    a. TRONC (trunk or box) system.
    b. LIFO system.
    c. tipping out system.
    d. FIFO system.

4. "Would you like a cocktail?" "Will you have dessert?" "Will you have an after-dinner liqueur?" These are all examples of:
    a. a soft sell.
    b. a hard sell.
    c. suggestive selling.
    d. the right way to sell.

5. Which of the following is not one of the seven commandments of customer service?
    a. Bend the rules.
    b. Lie if need be.
    c. Be a fantastic fixer.
    d. None of the above.

6. Oscar at the Waldorf Hotel in New York was a:
    a. server.
    b. manager.
    c. maitre d'.
    d. bell man.

7. The food order should be taken by:
    a. asking the senior female for her order first.
    b. asking the female that looks most ready for her order first.
    c. from left to right.
    d. from right to left.

8. What is the first thing a sever should do upon approaching a new table?
    a. suggest beverages.
    b. give the specials.
    c. introduce themselves.
    d. take a drink order.

9. What is the "hands-in-the-pocket" policy?
    a. no matter how obnoxious a patron becomes, never considers being physical in handling the situation.
    b. servers should keep there hands in their pockets when not taking an order.
    c. bussers and servers should always immediately put extra tips in their pockets when given to them from a guest.
    d. none of the above.

10. Who is known as the as the creator of Eggs Benedict, Veal Oscar and for aiding in the popularization of Thousand Island dressing?
    a. Charlie Trotter
    b. Julia Childs
    c. John Walker
    d. Oscar of the Waldorf

11. If a patron has the "Nothing is too good for our anniversary" attitude, the server should use:
    a. a soft sell.
    b. a hard sell.
    c. pressure.
    d. none of the above.

12. How many people should serve a party of six?
    a. one
    b. two
    c. three
    d. four

13. The first and last person the guest meets at a restaurant is the:
    a. server.
    b. manager.
    c. host/hostess.
    d. other guests.

14. Which of the following types of lighting is favorable in a dinner house?
    a. recessed lighting.
    b. bright lighting.
    c. high lighting.
    d. low lighting.

15. Servers can expect more problems from people:
    a. who come into a restaurant as a single.
    b. seated in open spaces.
    c. seated at booths.
    d. all the above.

SHORT ANSWER QUESTIONS

1. What are 3 characteristics of a good server? _____

_____

_____

_____

2. What is the best approach for handling a difficult guest? _____

_____

_____

_____

3. What are the seven commandments of customer service? _____

_____

_____

_____

_____

_____

4. What is the main responsibility of the host/hostesses job? _____

_____

_____

_____

5. Name 4 strategies for handling complaints._____

_____

_____

_____

CHAPTER 12: BAR AND BEVERAGES

OBJECTIVES

- Explain how to obtain an alcoholic beverage license.

- Identify factors to consider when developing the design and layout of a bar.

- List guidelines for suggesting wines to accompany menu items.

- Identify a restaurant's legal liability regarding the sale of alcoholic beverages.

- List ways in which bartenders and others can defraud the restaurant bar and beverage operation.

CHAPTER OUTLINE

Beverages
- Beverages account for 25%–30% of total sales.
  - A ratio higher than this will attract the Department of Alcoholic Beverage Control.
- The cost of beverage production is less than in the kitchen:
  - Consequently, the margins are greater.

Alcoholic Beverage Licenses
- ***On-sale general.*** Authorizes the sale of all types of alcoholic beverages—namely, beer, wine and distilled spirits—for consumption on the premises.
- ***Off-sale general.*** Authorizes the sale of all types of alcoholic beverages for consumption off the premises in original, sealed containers.
- ***On-sale beer and wine.*** Authorizes the sale on the premises of all types of beer, wine and malt liquor.
- ***Off-sale beer and wine.*** Authorizes the sale of all types of beer, wine and malt beverages for consumption off the premises in original containers.
- ***On-sale beer.*** Authorizes the sale on the licensed premises of beer and other malt beverages with an alcoholic content of 4% or less by weight.

How to Apply for a License
- The application process can be lengthy.
- States have jurisdiction over the sale of alcohol.
- State regulations must be met to be granted a license.
- Notices stating that a license has been applied for must be placed in the newspaper and posted in the window of the restaurant for a minimum of 30 days.
- There are 2 types of alcoholic beverage licenses:
  - General liquor license.
  - Beer and wine license.

Bar Layout and Design
- The overall design and layout of the restaurant.
- The intended prominence of the bar.
- The number of bartenders required to operate the bar and beverage service.
- The volume of business expected.
- The degree of self-sufficiency of the bar.
- The electric and water supply.
- The construction costs of providing electric and water supply.
- The distance to the storeroom and the dispensing system.
- The location of the beer kegs and cooling equipment.
- The type of restaurant.

Placement of the Bar within the Restaurant
- The bar should be in a location that has easy access.
- If you want the bar to be a highlight of the restaurant, place it near the entrance in prominent lighting.
- Some bars provide comfortable seating so the customers can relax.
- Seats placed close together encourage conversation.

The Speed Gun
- Used in bars as a pouring device that conveniently lets the bartender mix routine drinks.
- The average gun contains two sodas, a juice, soda water, ginger ale and tonic.
- A speed gun is located at each drink-making station.

Glass Washing
- Glasses may be washed by a machine, which is normally housed under the bar counter, or in a three-compartment sink.
- The reason for the three-compartment sink is sanitation:
  - The first sink has a brush, is filled with hot water, and has a special cleansing agent for bar glassware.
  - The middle sink has a clear, hot rinse.
  - The third sink has a sanitizing germicide agent.
  - A space with a rubber mat is provided for glasses to drain on.

Bartenders are Responsible for:
- Welcoming the guest, taking and preparing the drink and food orders in a friendly manner.
- Making sure that the drink is rung up and paid for.
- Keeping the bar and bar area clean, including glassware.
- Prepping enough fruit, juices, liquor and other stock for the shift.
- Replacing any used stock for the next shift.
- Cutting off or refusing to serve anyone who appears intoxicated, then making arrangements for the person to get home safely.
- Providing the guests with entertaining conversation.
- Making drinks for the servers and providing them with change.
- Taking inventory of all beer and liquor bottles at the end of shift.
- Remembering everyone's name!

Basic Inventory
- The selection of a basic bar inventory depends on the type of restaurant.
    - For example, a trendy upscale restaurant will carry several premium brands that a neighborhood Italian restaurant will not.

Wines
- Wine is the fermented juice of freshly gathered grapes.
- Wine is produced in many temperate parts of the world.
- The soil, climate and cultivation all have a significant impact on the wines character.
- Too much or too little of one essential element will mean a poor tasting wine.
- Wine is first categorized by color: red, white or rose, then are further classified as light beverage wines, still, sparkling, fortified, and aromatic.
- Wine is made in six steps:
    1. Crushing
    2. Fermenting
    3. Racking
    4. Maturing
    5. Filtering
    6. Bottling
- After maturing, the wine is filtered to help stabilize it and remove any solid particles still in the wine.
    - This process is called **fining.**
- The wine is then **clarified** by adding either egg white or bentonite, which removes impurities as it sinks to the bottom of the vat.
- Fine **vintage** wines are kept for a few years to further mature in the bottle and are consumed at their peak– several years later.
- White wines mature quicker than red and are often consumed within a few months of bottling.

Other Types of Wines:
- Sparkling
- Fortified
- Aromatic

Responsible Alcoholic Beverage Service
1. Write a responsible alcohol-serving mission statement outlining your position on drinking and safety. Once the mission is written down, the operator has a basis from which to complete the policy and plan.
2. Review local and state liquor laws.
3. Assess the operation's clientele.
4. Make a plan for developing and maintaining relationships with law enforcement officials and transportation organizations.
5. Establish a comprehensive program of ongoing staff training.
6. Create a schedule of management audits of policy and practice.
7. Create a system of actions that demonstrate support for responsible and enjoyable drinking.

Alcoholic Beverage Service
- A trained person at the door to check ID's, to discourage patrons from leaving with alcohol.
- Encourage "designated driver" program.
- Post taxi numbers next to pay phone.
- Encourage food consumption.

Controls
- Liquor inventory that is not properly controlled can seriously affect the restaurant.
- It is safe to assume that given chance, liquor will be stolen.
- Institute a weekly or biweekly audit.
  - This may be done by an outside auditor, which is recommended for larger and higher-volume restaurants, or internally, with the correct equipment.

Controlling Loses
- Limit bar access to bartenders and make them accountable for the pouring cost results.
- Give incentive bonuses for good results.
- Require drink orders to be rung into the register before the drinks are made.
- Use a remote system.
- Install a video system and alarm on the back door.
- Do not allow bags in the bar area.
- Provide lockers in another area.
- If mistakes are made have them written off and signed for by management.
- Cushion bar floors to reduce breakage.
- Set up a system that allows employees to anonymously report incidents.
- Be careful in hiring employees for the beverage operation; check references and do background checks.

Practice Quiz

TRUE OR FALSE
On the following questions, answer whether the statement provided is true or false.

T   F   1.   Today, a reasonable sales split is about 25 to 30 percent beverage sales and 70 to 75 percent food sales.

T   F   2.   Textures are the qualities in food and wine that we feel in the mouth, such as softness, smoothness, roundness, richness, thinness, creaminess, chewiness, oiliness, harshness, and so on.

T   F   3.   An on-sale general license authorizes the sale of all types of alcoholic beverages for consumption off the premises in original, sealed containers.

T   F   4.   The speed rack holds all of the top shelf liquor.

T   F   5. In the food and beverage industry, it is estimated that 50 percent of employees steal regardless of the controls in place

T   F   6. Each state has a Department of Alcoholic Beverage Control.

T   F   7. To avoid or solve liquor control problems, owners should institute a daily audit.

T   F   8. The legislation that governs the sale of alcoholic beverages is called dream stop litigation.

T   F   9. Flavors are food and beverage elements perceived by the olfactory nerves as fruity, minty, herbal, nutty, cheesy, smoky, flowery, earthy, and so on.

T   F 10. For restaurants, there are three main kinds of alcoholic beverage licenses.

FILL IN THE BLANKS: KEY TERM REVIEW
On the following questions, fill in the blank with the most appropriate key term.

1.   By creating a convivial place for _____, restaurateurs can offer a place for relaxation, socialization, and entertainment.

2.   The bar setup is divided into three areas: the _____, the_____, and the _____.

3.   _____ is the fermented juice of freshly gathered grapes.

4.   The _____ is used in bars as a pouring device that conveniently lets the bartender mix routine drinks.

5.   The main equipment in the under bar is the speed rack, which contains the _____ brand liquors.

6.   After maturing, the wine is filtered to help stabilize it and remove any solid particles still in the wine. This process is called _____.

7.   Sherries, Ports, Madeira's, and Marsala's are _____, meaning they have had brandy or wine alcohol added to them.

8.   Wine is _____ by adding either egg white or bentonite, which removes impurities as it sinks to the bottom of the vat.

9.   The name and logo of the beer is usually displayed on a _____, supplied by the distributor and located in view of the guests on the bar counter or, occasionally, on the back bar counter.

10. The _____, usually the back wall of the bar—is for aesthetics and functions as a storage and display area.

MULTIPLE CHOICE QUESTIONS: CONCEPT REVIEW
On the following questions, circle the choice that best answers the question.

1. In order for any sparkling wing to be called "Champagne" it must come from:
    a. Italy.
    b. Portugal.
    c. California.
    d. France.

2. Which of the following licenses authorizes the sale on the premises of all types of beer, wine, and malt liquor?
    a. Off-sale beer and wine
    b. On-sale general
    c. Off-sale general
    d. On-sale beer and wine

3. Where does one apply for a liquor license?
    a. ServSafe
    b. The state liquor authority
    c. The District Court House
    d. The National Restaurant Association

4. The main equipment in the under bar is the:
    a. premium-brand liquors.
    b. well brand liquors.
    c. speed rack.
    d. b and c

5. Wine is first categorized by:
    a. smell.
    b. color.
    c. region.
    d. type (i.e. still, sparkling, fortified, etc.).

6. Red wine gains its color during which of the following processes?
    a. crushing.
    b. racking.
    c. fermentation.
    d. filtering.

7. Which of the following licenses authorizes the sale of all types of alcoholic beverages for consumption off the premises in original, sealed containers?

a. Off-sale beer and wine
b. On-sale general
c. Off-sale general
d. On-sale beer and wine

8. After maturing, the wine is filtered to help stabilize it and remove any solid particles still in the wine. This process is called
   a. fining.
   b. filtering.
   c. fermentation.
   d. racking.

9. Sherries, Ports, Madeira's, and Marsala's are fortified wines, meaning they:
   a. are fermented for a longer period than any other type of wine.
   b. are fermented for a shorter period than any other type of wine.
   c. are flavored with herbs, roots, flowers, and barks.
   d. have had brandy or wine alcohol added to them.

10. The second step in the winemaking process is:
    a. crushing.
    b. racking.
    c. fermentation.
    d. filtering.

11. The more popular varietal red wines include all but which of the following?
    a. Cabernet Sauvignon
    b. Zinfandel
    c. Merlot
    d. Pinot Grigio

12. Which of the following licenses authorizes the sale of all types of alcoholic beverages—namely, beer, wine, and distilled spirits—for consumption on the premises?
    a. Off-sale beer and wine
    b. On-sale general
    c. Off-sale general
    d. On-sale beer

13. The Director of Alcoholic Beverage Control heads the department and is appointed by the:
    a. governor.
    b. state attorney.
    c. president.
    d. superintendent.

14. Some elements of creating a responsible alcoholic beverage program are:
    a. Write a responsible alcoholic serving mission statement on your position on drinking and safety.
    b. Review local and state laws.

c. Establish a comprehensive program of ongoing staff training and management audits.
d. All of the above.

15. Beverage sales yield:
   a. more profit than food sales.
   b. less than profit food sales.
   c. the same profit than food sales.
   d. more production costs than food sales.

SHORT ANSWER QUESTIONS

1. List the 6 steps of the wine making process. _____

_____

_____

_____

2. Briefly describe what happens during each of the steps you listed above? _____

_____

_____

_____

_____

_____

_____

_____

3. What makes a wine "vintage"? _____

_____

_____

_____

4. Name 5 main responsibilities of a bartender? _____

_____

_____

_____

_____

5. What should a bartender do if a guest suddenly appears intoxicated? _____

_____

_____

_____

_____

_____

CHAPTER 13: RESTAURANT TECHNOLOGY

OBJECTIVES

- Identify the main types of restaurant industry technologies.

- List and describe the main types of software programs.

- Identify factors to consider when choosing technology for a restaurant.

CHAPTER OUTLINE

Technology in the Restaurant Industry
- Technology has come a long way from the mom-and-pop operators and their proverbial cigar box!
- Independent operators may not require—or be able to afford—the sophistication of technology that chain operators are using.
- It is hard to overlook the progress in making technology available and affordable for independent restaurants.

Back-of-the-House Technology
- Back-of-the-house, or back-office, restaurant technology consists of:
  - Product management systems for purchasing
  - Managing inventories
  - Menu management
  - Controlling labor and other costs
  - Tip reporting
  - Food and beverage cost percentages
  - Human resources
  - Financial reporting
- Purchasing: Product management tracks products through each inventory cycle and automatically reorders when the item falls below par stock.
  - The ingredients for the cost of recipes are calculated for total cost and selling prices.
- Inventory Control: Systems aid inventory control by quickly recording inventory and easily allowing new stock to be added.
- Food Costing:
  - When calculating the food and beverage cost percentage, a hand-held device (PDA) can enter the inventory amounts into the system.
  - Laser bar code scanning is speeding up the inventory-taking process and making it more accurate.
    - When the data is entered into the system, a variance report is generated and any significant variances are investigated.

- Food Costing:
  - ChefTec and ChefTec Plus software solutions integrate programs with recipe/menu costing, inventory control and nutritional analysis capabilities.

Menu Management
- MenuLink: Evaluates managers' produce purchasing, compares actual to expected food usage, tests proposed recipes and pricing changes.
  - The menu management function is used to determine what offers work best, so that coupon building may be directed toward those items.
  - Includes an Automated Raw Material Transfer: When one store needs to borrow material from another store, a transfer is generated.

Labor Management Systems
- Interfaces back and front-of-the-house working hours and human resources information.
- Handles human resources information.
- Includes module to monitor applications, recruitment, personnel information, I-9 status, tax status, availability, vacation information, benefit information, handles scheduling based on the forecasted volume of business for each meal period.
  - Examples: Windows-based labor schedulers and TimePro.

Financial Reporting
- Front-of-the-house and back-of- the-house systems may interface by transferring data to and from the central server.
  - This makes it easier for management to monitor service times, POS food costs, labor costs and guest counts.

E-learning
- Computer based training delivered via internet or proprietary.
- The National Restaurant Association Educational Foundation has several online courses (Example: ServSafe Food Safety Training Program).

Front-of-the-House Technology
- Revolves around the POS System.
  - Point of Sale System.
- Human Factors Engineering (HFE) focuses on:
  - Store performance.
  - User interface design.

Selection of POS Systems
- Aloha: Full range of restaurant products including Table Service and Virtual Order Processing.
- ASI: Popular Restaurant Manager POS and Write-On Handheld.
- IBM: Linux servers and Sure POS 700 series.
- Sharp: UP-5900 system combined with Maitre'D.
- NCR: 7454 POS Workstation- MS DOS and Windows certified.
- Micros: Eclipse PC Workstation.

- POS systems have come down in price.
- They offer the independent restaurateur the convenience of providing information for financials that obviates the need for cash registers and spreadsheets.
- The cost of installing a POS system will depend on the number of stations required.
  - A 125-seat casual dining restaurant could use two or three stations in the dining area, one in the bar and printers in the kitchen, plus a managers' station.
  - The total cost would be in the $18,000 to $20,000 range.
- POS systems have come down in price.
- They offer the independent restaurateur the convenience of providing information for financials that obviates the need for cash registers and spreadsheets.
- The cost of installing a POS system will depend on the number of stations required.
  - A 125-seat casual dining restaurant could use two or three stations in the dining area, one in the bar and printers in the kitchen, plus a managers' station.
  - The total cost would be in the $18,000 to $20,000 range.

Guest Services and Websites
- Restaurant technology has evolved to the point where a restaurant can store and recall guests' preferences for tables, menu items, wines, and servers.
- Additional advances include:
  - Internet Booking
  - Guest Checks- Splitting and Suggested Tip Amounts
  - High Speed Internet Access
  - User Friendly Web Sites
  - Wireless Surveys

Practice Quiz

TRUE OR FALSE
On the following questions, answer whether the statement provided is true or false.

T F 1. When calculating the food and beverage cost percentage, a hand-held device called a PDA can enter the inventory amounts into the system.

T F 2. ChefTec and ChefTec Plus software solutions integrate programs with recipe and menu costing, inventory control, and nutritional analysis capabilities.

T F 3. There is a definite link between food costing and menu management.

T F 4. Labor management systems only interface back-of-the-house employee working hours.

T F 5. The point-of-sale terminal is the workhorse of restaurant operations.

T F 6. POS systems are continuing to increase in price.

T　F　7. Aloha's virtual order processing communicates between the kitchen and wait staff.

T　F　8. Restaurant web sites need an appealing, user-friendly design and functionality, including accessibility and interactivity.

T　F　9. Computer-based training is decreasing in the workplace.

T　F　10. Most restaurants divide their technology into two parts: back and front of the house.

FILL IN THE BLANKS: KEY TERM REVIEW
On the following questions, fill in the blank with the most appropriate key term.

1.　Among the many operations, _____technology consists of product management systems for purchasing, managing inventories, menu management, controlling labor and other costs.

2.　When calculating the food and beverage cost percentage, a hand-held device, called a _____, can enter the inventory amounts into the system.

3.　_____ include a module to monitor applications tax forms, vacation, benefit information, and do the scheduling based on the forecasted volume of business for each meal period.

4.　The _____ terminal is the workhorse of restaurant operations.

5.　MenuLinks _____ function is used to determine what offers work best, so that coupon building may be directed toward those items.

6.　Computer-based training, known as _____, is delivered via the Internet or proprietary Internet sites.

MULTIPLE CHOICE QUESTIONS: CONCEPT REVIEW
On the following questions, circle the choice that best answers the question.

1.　Back-of-the-house, or back-office, restaurant technology consists of:
a. product management systems for purchasing, managing inventories, menu management, controlling labor and other costs.
b. the point-of-sale (POS) system and wireless handheld devices.
c. guest service.
d. a and b

2.　Back-office systems aid inventory control by quickly recording the inventory and easily allowing new stock to be added. This is called:
a. food costing.
b. purchasing.

c. inventory control.

d. labor management.

3. The handheld device used to enter inventory amounts into the system is called a:

a. PDA.

b. LAN.

c. POS.

d. SQL.

4. MenuLink's menu management function is used to:

a. determine what offers work best for couponing.

b. take inventory.

c. make schedules.

d. determine liquor costs.

5. Which of the following is the workhorse of restaurant operations?

a. PDA

b. LAN

c. POS

d. SQL

6. Which of the following concentrates on restaurant performance improvements allowing the restaurant operator to identify areas in which to increase revenues, improve operational efficiency, and improve guest service?

a. MCO

b. HFE

c. EEG

d. none of the above

7. Darden Restaurants recently introduced a _____ software system that employees use to access benefits and other information through its intranet site.

a. ServSafe

b. PeopleSoft

c. Bar Code

d. MenuLink

8. Technological improvements have made it possible to do a restaurant's food cost percentage in about _____ of the time it used to take and with more accuracy.

a. one-quarter

b. half

c. one-third

d. three-quarters

9. When a restaurant's employees are not productive and customer-service levels are not up to snuff, such problems can often be traced to the design of the _____ interface, ranging from complicated screen layouts to inappropriately sized buttons and the poor use of colors for different menu items.
   a. PDA
   b. POS
   c. HFE
   d. SQL

10. All front-of-the-house employees should take the _____ courses and all back-of-the-house employees should take the _____ courses offered by the National Restaurant Association Educational Foundation.
   a. Bar Code, ServSafe
   b. ServSafe, PeopleSoft,
   c. Bar Code, PeopleSoft
   d. ServSafe, Bar Code

11. About ___ percent of Fortune 1000 companies have significant e-learning initiatives underway.
   a. 65
   b. 75
   c. 85
   d. 95

12. Easy access to restaurant web sites is importation, it is also important to include:
   a. menu and beverage lists.
   b. directions and parking information.
   c. the managers personal contact number.
   d. a and b

13. When calculating the food and beverage cost percentage, using a hand-held device to enter the inventory amounts into the system is called:
   a. food costing.
   b. purchasing.
   c. inventory control.
   d. labor control.

14. NCR offers a Human Factors engineering team to:
   a. provide quantitative data for evaluating current store performance levels and user interface design.
   b. concentrate on restaurant improvements that allow a restaurant operator to identify specific areas.
   c. allow the operator to improve operational efficiency and guest service.
   d. all of the above.

15. Back office systems aide inventory control by:
    a. quickly recording the inventory and easily allowing new stock to be added.
    b. automatically controlling the inventory everyday.
    c. recommending price increases as product prices increase.
    d. All of the above.

SHORT ANSWER QUESTIONS

1. TimePro from Commeg Systems has a time, attendance, and scheduling feature. What is the purpose of this feature? _____

_____

_____

_____

2. What do labor management systems include? _____

_____

_____

_____

3. What does Cambridge Investments use MenuLink for? _____

_____

_____

_____

4. MenuLink has developed a new feature for its Back Office Assistant called the Automated Raw Material Transfer. What does this feature perform? _____

_____

_____

_____

CHAPTER 14: BUDGETING AND CONTROLLING COSTS

OBJECTIVES

- Describe front-of-the-house operations.

- Describe back-of-the-house operations.

- Identify ways to control food, beverage, and labor costs.

- Discuss methods of guest check control.

CHAPTER OUTLINE

Front-of-the-House Operations
- Front of the house refers to the hosts, bartenders, servers and bussers.
- The visual appeal of the building and parking area are important to potential guests.
  - Guests receive a first impression known as curbside appeal—or, would you even stop or get out of the car?
- The first thing restaurant managers do is to forecast how many guests are expected and share that information with the kitchen.
- A guest count is arrived at by taking the same day last year and factoring in things like today's weather, day of the week, and so on.
- The elements of management are planning, organizing, communicating, decision-making, motivation and control.
- Schedules and checklists help organize the restaurant.
- A "lead sheet" lists staff on both shifts so you can easily see who is on duty.

Back-of-the-House Operations
- The back of the house is sometimes called the "heart" of the operation.
- The kitchen is the center of production.
- Production sheets are created for each station, detailing all the tasks necessary to bring the food quantities up to par stock of prepared items and to complete the preparation on time.
- The chef makes sure that all menu items are prepared in accordance with the standardized recipes and that the line is ready for service.
- During service, either the chef or a manager may act as a caller—in an attempt to control the ordering and expediting of plates at the pass.

Control
- There is so much food and beverage in a restaurant that, unless management and owners exert tight control, losses will occur.
- Restaurants can use programs like ChefTec, which shows the actual food cost compared with the ideal food cost. This is known as food optimization.

- The food cost percentage should be calculated at least monthly:
  - The formula for doing the food cost percentage is Cost/Sales × 100
- Control of liquor is critical to the success of the restaurant.
- Management decides on the selling price and mark-up for beer, wine, and liquor.
  - This will set the standard for the beverage cost percentage.
  - Normal pouring cost for beer is 24 to 25%.
  - Wine should have a pouring cost of 26 to 30%.
  - Liquor pouring costs should be 16 to 20% of sales.
  - Combined, the beverage pouring cost should be 23 to 25% of beverage sales.

Controllable Expenses
- Term used to describe the various expenses that can be changed in the short term:
  - Variable costs
  - Payroll
  - Operating expenses
  - Marketing
  - Heat
  - Light
  - Repairs
  - Maintenance

Labor Costs
- Depending on the type of restaurant and the degree of service provided, labor costs may range from approximately 16% of sales in a quick-service restaurant to 24% in a casual operation and up to about 30% in an upscale restaurant.
- Projecting payroll costs requires the preparation of staffing schedules and establishing wage rates.
- Staffing patterns may vary during different periods of the year, with changes occurring seasonally or when there are other sales variations.
- Payroll and related costs fall into two categories:
  - Variable (percentage ratio to payroll).
  - Fixed (dollar amount per employee on the payroll).
- Variable items include those mandated by law: Social Security, unemployment insurance, Workers' Compensation insurance and state disability insurance.
- The fixed items usually mean employee benefits and include health insurance, union welfare insurance, life insurance and other employee benefits.

Guest Check Control
- Without check control, a server can give food and beverages away or sell it and keep the income.
- Guest checks can be altered and substitutions made if the checks are not numbered.
  - To avoid such temptations, most restaurants require that the server sign for checks as received and return those not used at the end of the shift.
- For tight control, every guest check is audited, additions checked, and every check accounted for by number.
- Some operators control restaurant income by having servers act as their own cashiers.

- They bring their own banks of $50 in change; they do not operate from a cash register but out of their own pockets; they deposit their income in a night box at the bank.

Productivity Analysis and Cost Control
- Without knowing what each expense item should be as a ratio of gross sales, the manager is at a distinct disadvantage.
- The simplest employee productivity measure is sales generated per employee per year:
  - Divide the number of full-time equivalent employees into the gross sales for the year.

Practice Quiz

TRUE OR FALSE
On the following questions, answer whether the statement provided is true or false.

T F 1. The visual appeal of the building and parking area are important to potential guests.

T F 2. Restaurants can use programs like ChefTec, which shows the actual food cost compared with the ideal food cost. This is known as *food optimization.*

T F 3. One of the more complicated employee productivity measures is sales generated per employee per year.

T F 4. Labor is the largest controllable cost.

T F 5. The variable cost items usually include things such as employee benefits and health insurance.

T F 6. Beverage inventory is done by "eyeball," measuring bottles of liquor in tenths.

T F 7. Combined, the beverage pouring cost should be 10 to 15 percent of beverage sales.

T F 8. Variable costs are normally controllable.

T F 9. Employee meals are treated as a taxable benefit by the IRS.

T F 10. For tight control, every guest check is audited, additions checked, and every check accounted for by number.

FILL IN THE BLANKS: KEY TERM REVIEW
On the following questions, fill in the blank with the most appropriate key term.

1. _____ is the term used to describe the expenses that can be changed in the short term.

2. In most full-service restaurants, the largest variable is _____.

3. The hot plate area where plated items are passed to the food-servers is known as the _____.

4. The chef makes out a _____ for each station, detailing all the tasks necessary to bring the food quantities up to par stock of prepared items and to complete the preparation on time.

5. The _____ cycle begins with management deciding which brands to have for the well or house, then setting a par stock of beverages to have on hand.

6. In the _____ are the areas that include purchasing, receiving, storage, issuing, food preparation and service, dishwashing area, sanitation, accounting, budgeting, and control.

7. Goals are set for each _____. For example, sales goals include the number of guests per meal every day and the average check.

8. The selling price and mark-up for beer, wine, and liquor will set the standard for the _____.

9. _____ refers to the hosts, bartenders, servers, and bussers.

10. A _____ is arrived at by taking the same day last year and factoring in things like today's weather, day of the week, and so on.

MULTIPLE CHOICE QUESTIONS: CONCEPT REVIEW
On the following questions, circle the choice that best answers the question.

1. The normal pouring cost for beer is:
   a. 10 percent.
   b. 15 percent.
   c. 20 percent.
   d. 25 percent.

2. Liquor pouring costs should be ___ to ___ percent of sales.
   a. 10 to15
   b. 16 to 20
   c. 25 to 30
   d. 30 to 35

3.   In most full-service restaurants, the largest variable is:
     a. labor costs.
     b. food costs.
     c. beverage costs.
     d. benefits.

4.   Who is at "the pass"?
     a. the chef
     b. the manager
     c. the server
     d. a or b

5.   Several restaurants use the _____ to assist in managing the restaurant—it aids from planning to control.
     a. Red Book
     b. Blue Book
     c. Black Book
     d. Yellow Book

6.   Hosts, bartenders, servers, and bussers are all part of the:
     a. front of the house.
     b. back of the house.
     c. guest experience.
     d. a and c.

7.   Which of the following lists the staff on both shifts of the day so you can easily see who's on duty?
     a. prep sheet
     b. lead sheet
     c. production sheet
     d. forecasting sheet

8.   Ideally, the chef, having set the menu for the day checks inventory at _____ to ensure sufficient food quantities.
     a. the close the night before.
     b. the opening the day of.
     c. the beginning of the shift.
     d. opening the day before.

9.   Which of the following details all the tasks necessary to bring the food quantities of prepared items up to par stock and to complete the preparation on time?
     a. prep. sheet
     b. lead sheet
     c. production sheet
     d. forecasting sheet

10. Restaurants can use programs like ChefTec, which shows the actual food cost compared with the ideal food cost. This is known as food:
    a. control.
    b. mixing.
    c. optimization.
    d. planning.

11. The first thing restaurant managers do at the beginning of a shift is to:
    a. assign server stations.
    b. forecast how many guests are expected.
    c. get a coffee.
    d. give a service meeting.

12. Which of the following people does not need to spend time with guests?
    a. managers
    b. cooks
    c. servers
    d. a and b

13. Who is responsible for checking on the expected level of business—based on the prior year's business?
    a. the opening manager
    b. the closing manager
    c. the chef
    d. the servers

14. For a 30 percent cost, if a bottle of wine cost $10.00, the selling price is:
    a. $30.
    b. $33.
    c. $40.
    d. $44.

15. Taking the same day last year and factoring in things like today's weather, day of the week and so on, are all parts of arriving at a:
    a. yearly report.
    b. semi-annual report.
    c. guest count.
    d. sales ratio.

SHORT ANSWER QUESTIONS

1. Define controllable expenses. _____

_____

_____

_____

2. Give five examples of controllable expenses. _____

_____

_____

_____

3. What is the formula for doing the food cost percentage? _____

_____

_____

_____

4. What are the 2 categories payroll costs fall into? _____

_____

_____

_____

CHAPTER 15: ORGANIZATION, RECRUITING AND STAFFING

OBJECTIVES

- Describe the processes for creating job and task analyses.

- Describe the components of a job description, and list the guidelines for creating one.

- Identify legal issues surrounding hiring and employment.

- Determine the legality of potential interview questions.

CHAPTER OUTLINE

Task and Job Analysis
- Task: A related sequence of work.
- Job: A series of related responsibilities.
- Job Analysis: Detailed examination of tasks and jobs to be performed.
- Job Specification: Identifies the skills and qualifications needed to perform the job.
- Bottom-Up Method: Most frequently used when the organization already exists.
    - The work behavior of the employees is the basis for analysis (e.g., shortcuts).
- Top-Down Method: Used when opening a new restaurant.
    - Missions, goals and objectives are examined to determine what tasks must be performed.

Guidelines for a Job Description
- Job Title; reports to; location.
- Describe the job, not the person in the job.
- Describe the performance standards: What is expected as a result of doing the required work.
- Give a copy of the evaluation form for the job to the employee.
- Be sure that the requirements listed support the essential function of the job.
- Do not describe in fine detail.
- Sentences should be short, simple and to the point.
- If technical jargon is used, explain it.
- The description should be detailed enough to include all aspects of the job.
- Include the amount of time to do each job function.
- Describe the job setting or environment.

Job Specification
- Lists the education and technical/conceptual skills a person needs to satisfactorily perform the requirements of the job.
    - Once the tasks performed in a job are described, a separate section of the job description form can be developed.

Job Instruction Sheet
- Task analysis can be converted into job instructions.
  - These serve as a guide for new employees and as a quality assurance measure for the maintenance of work standards.

Organizing People and Jobs
- Every restaurant is organized so that the following restaurant functions are performed:
  - Human resources management and supervision.
  - Food and beverage purchasing.
  - Receiving, storing and issuing.
  - Food preparation.
  - Foodservice.
  - Food cleaning; dish and utensil washing.
  - Marketing/sales.
  - Promotion, advertising and public relations.
  - Accounting and auditing.
  - Bar service.

Staffing the Restaurant
- Recruitment, pre-employment testing, interviewing, selection, employment, placement, orientation and training are key words in finding the right people and preparing them to work successfully in the restaurant.

Recruitment
- Prospective employees are attracted to the restaurant in order for a suitable applicant to be selected for employment.
- This must be carried out in accordance to federal and state employment laws.

Pre-employment Testing
- Must be valid and reliable.
  - A valid test measures what it is supposed to measure.
  - A reliable test shows the same results with repeated testing.
- There is a range of tests to select from (i.e. intelligence, aptitude, and achievement).
- Some restaurants test for substance abuse and honesty, and some use psychological tests to select the best possible employees.

Interviewing
- The purpose of the interview is to:
  - Gain sufficient information to determine that the applicant is capable of doing the job.
  - Give information about the company and the job.
  - Ask appropriate "legal but leading" questions.

Ideal Employee Profiles
- Employees constitute a large part of the restaurant's ambiance, spirit and efficiency.
- Employees must fit into the job

- Outgoing personalities fit well in the front of the house.
- It is important to give employees a chance to succeed in the restaurant.

Selection
- Determining the eligibility and suitability of a perspective employee (how well they will do the job and how well they will fit in with the team).
- Personal appearance, grooming, and hygiene are also important.
- The purpose is to hire an employee that will be a team player and exceed expectations.

Employment of Minors
- Several leading restaurant chains have found that teenagers, beginning at age 16, are excellent candidates for almost every restaurant job, from bussing and dishwashing to cooking and order taking.
- A number of federal regulations control the kind of work permissible for minors (under age 16).
- There are age restrictions stating the maximum amount of hours a minor may work.

The Multiple Interview Approach
- During the first interview, the candidate may be given a rating of 1 to 5.
- Only those rating a 5 are given an additional interview with a second interviewer.

Three Main Hiring Objectives
- Hire people who project an image and attitude appropriate for your restaurant.
- Hire people who will work with you rather than spend their time fighting your rules, procedures, and system.
- Hire people whose personal and financial requirements are a good fit with the hours and positions you are hiring for.

Practice Quiz

TRUE OR FALSE
On the following questions, answer whether the statement provided is true or false.

T   F   1. Equal employment opportunity (EEO) is recruitment, selection and promotion practices, which are open, competitive and based on merit.

T   F   2. Several leading restaurant chains have found that teenagers, beginning at age 13, are excellent candidates for almost every restaurant job

T   F   3. Task analysis can be converted into job instructions, which can serve not only as a guide to new employees but also as a quality assurance measure.

T   F   4. The top down method is most frequently used when creating a task and/or job analysis in an organization that already exists and the work behavior of the existing employees is the basis for analysis.

T   F   5.   Acquired Immune Deficiency Syndrome (AIDS) cannot be transmitted through the air, water, or food.

T   F   6.   The bottom up method must be used when creating a task and/or job analysis in new restaurants because there are no existing employees to analyze.

T   F   7.   The National Restaurant Association spells out the work that may not be done by minors under 18 years of age.

T   F   8.   The Immigration Reform and Control Act of 1986 makes it legal for employers to employ undocumented aliens.

T   F   9.   The most useful source of employees is referrals by reliable present employees.

T   F   10.   One out of five Americans is considered disabled, according to the Census Bureau.

FILL IN THE BLANKS: KEY TERM REVIEW

On the following questions, fill in the blank with the most appropriate key term.

1.   The _____ prohibits discrimination against employees who are disabled and requires making "readily achievable" modifications in work practices and working conditions that enable them to work.

2.   _____ is the process of determining the eligibility and suitability of a prospective employee—not only how well a person can cook or serve, but also how he or she will fit in with the team.

3.   A _____ lists the education and technical/conceptual skills a person needs to satisfactorily perform the requirements of the job.

4.   _____ is the process by which prospective employees are attracted to the restaurant in order that a suitable applicant may be selected for employment.

5.   A _____ is a related sequence of work.

6.   Fundamental to the entire human resource function is _____ and _____, the examination in detail of the tasks and jobs to be performed.

7.   _____ identifies the qualifications and skills needed to perform the job.

8.   A _____ is a series of related responsibilities.

9.   _____ seeks to identify certain behavioral characteristics that may determine successful employment practices.

10. _____ state that employers may not discriminate in employment on the basis of an individual's race, religion, color, sex, national origin, marital status, age, veteran status, family relationship, disabilities, or juvenile record that has been expunged.

MULTIPLE CHOICE QUESTIONS: CONCEPT REVIEW

On the following questions, circle the choice that best answers the question.

1. When a series of related responsibilities are written down in an organized form, they constitute a:
   a. task analysis.
   b. job specifications.
   c. job description.
   d. job analysis.

2. A person can be thought of as a clean-up person, but a better description would be "a person who expedites seat turnover." This is an example of emphasizing the:
   a. task analysis.
   b. job description.
   c. job objective.
   d. none of the above.

3. Who is responsible for all food preparation and supervision of kitchen staff?
   a. Pantry Supervisor
   b. Bookkeeper
   c. Storeroom Supervisor
   d. Food Production Manager

4. On school days, minors of what age may only work a maximum of 3 hours per day, 18 hours per week; on nonschool days, 8 hours per day, 40 hours per week?
   a. 12 and 13
   b. 13 and 14
   c. 14 and 15
   d. 15 and 16

5. According to the Census Bureau _____ out of _____ employees are considered disabled.
   a. 1, 3
   b. 1, 4
   c. 1, 5
   d. 1, 6

6. A first interview may be given and the candidate rated from 1 to 5 on whatever factors are considered relevant to successful job performance. Only those candidates receiving a rating of 5 are given an additional appointment with a second interviewer. This is the:
   a. public interview approach.
   b. multiple interview approach.
   c. single interview approach.
   d. private interview approach.

7. Which method of job analysis must be used in new restaurants because there are no existing employees to analyze?
   a. bottom-up
   b. top-up
   c. bottom-down
   d. top-down

8. Who is responsible for clearing the tables, re-setting them with fresh linens and eating utensils, fills water glasses, and helps in other housekeeping chores in the dining area?
   a. Server
   b. Assistant Manager
   c. Bus Person
   d. Dining Room Manager

9. Several leading restaurant chains have found that teenagers, beginning at age ___, are excellent candidates for almost every restaurant job
   a. 14
   b. 15
   c. 16
   d. 17

10. Minors of what age may not work before 7 a.m. or after 7 p.m. on school days; from June 1 through Labor Day, they may work until 9 p.m.?
    a. 12 and 13
    b. 13 and 14
    c. 14 and 15
    d. 15 and 16

11. The most useful source of employees is:
    a. referrals by reliable present employees.
    b. classified ads.
    c. job fairs.
    d. local partnerships.

12. At age ___, teenagers may legally work at any job.
    a. 15
    b. 16
    c. 17
    d. 18

13. Who is responsible for coordinating dining room activities, training and supervising the host/hostess, waiters, waitresses, busboys, and busgirls?
    a. Pantry Supervisor
    b. Dining Room Manager
    c. Assistant Manager
    d. Food Production Manager

14. Which of the following comprise a list of the work steps performed, arranged in sequential order if there is a natural cycle to the work?
    a. Task analysis
    b. Job instructions
    c. Job Analysis
    d. Job specification

15. When the organization already exists and the work behavior of the existing employees can be the basis for job analysis which approach would be used?
    a. bottom-up
    b. top-up
    c. bottom-down
    d. top-down

SHORT ANSWER QUESTIONS

1. Discuss the three main hiring objectives in the text. _____

_____

_____

_____

2. What is the purpose of a job specification? _____

_____

_____

_____

3. What is the goal of a job interview? _____

_____

_____

_____

4. What happens during the process of selection? _____

_____

_____

_____

CHAPTER 16: EMPLOYEE TRAINING AND DEVELOPMENT

OBJECTIVES

- List the goals of an orientation program.

- Compare and contrast behavior modeling and learner-controlled instruction.

- List guidelines for effective trainers.

- Describe characteristics of effective managers.

- Describe elements of an effective training program.

CHAPTER OUTLINE

Eight Goals of Orientation
1. To explain the company's history, philosophy, mission, goals and objectives.
2. To make the employee feel welcome.
3. To let employees know why they have been selected.
4. To ensure that the employee knows what to do and who to ask when unsure.
5. To explain and show what is expected.
6. To have employees explain and demonstrate each task.
7. To explain various programs and social activities available.
8. To show where everything is kept.

Training
- Most training programs involve comprehensive step-by-step job learning that utilize job checklists and differing styles of management control.
- Training programs also tend to emphasize varying types of sales incentives.
- The efficient approach to training is to analyze the job, break it down into the tasks performed and teach the tasks in the sequence in which they are normally performed.
- Management decides how extensive written job instructions should be.
- Being brief is an asset.
    - If the job tasks can be printed on a pocket-sized card, the employee has a handy reference.
- Guidelines for a job can be put together and given to the new employee to augment more comprehensive, detailed job instructions.

Behavior Modeling
- Depicts the right way to...
    - Handle personnel. problems.
    - Interview.
    - Evaluate applicants.
    - Make decisions.

- Emphasis on interpersonal skills—*people handling*—has always been of great importance in the restaurant or in any management position, but the move to deemphasize theory and emphasize "how to do" is new.
- Systematic exposure to models favored by an organization constitutes the training.
- Audiovisual materials in which an actor or company executive demonstrates the correct or approved techniques for dealing with problems are used by several foodservice companies.

Learner Controlled Instruction
- A program in which employees are given job standards to achieve and are asked to reach the standards at their own pace.
- Many people believe that it is less costly than classroom instruction.
- LCI accepts that people have different levels of ability.
- The learner is self-motivated and can proceed from unit to unit at a speed with which he or she is comfortable.
- Learning resources include books, written policies and practices, as well as experts.

The Manager as Coach
- Trains and motivates.
- Shows people how to perform.
- Gives criticism when needed.
- Stresses the RIGHT WAY.
- Gives positive feedback.

Leadership
- Transforms problems into challenges.
- Excites the imagination.
- Calls on pride.
- Develops a sense of accomplishment.
- Provides opportunities to overcome obstacles.

Characteristics of Effective Managers
- They continuously try to better past performance and compete with other restaurants.
- Rather than resting on past laurels, they never let themselves become too comfortable in their job.
- They are problem solvers and enjoy challenges.
- They are flexible and adapt to change.
- They anticipate future problems, rehearsing coming events in their minds.
- They do not cry over spilled milk or hold trials to place blame for what went wrong.
- They seek responsibility.
- They handle rejection or temporary failure without becoming unduly discouraged.
- They are not perfectionists; however, they can act in the absence of complete information and allow others the latitude to reach common goals in their own way.
- They perceive people as ends, not means.
- They take responsibility for employees.
- They build employee independence and initiative.

- They communicate confidence in themselves and the enterprise.
- They remember that they are the role models and that employees quickly pick up their habits, values, concern for others, and determination to get things done.
- They have concern and compassion for employee well-being.
- They lead by example, with consistency and fairness.
- They aim to motivate employees.

Subtleties of Supervision
- Management experts urge that employees be informed of what is important to the manager, the things the manager feels will make the department, manager and employee a success.

Motivation Through Partial Ownership
- *A piece of the action* is the term used by some restaurants in encouraging unit managers to acquire, through purchase, a percentage of the store they manage.
- The incentive of ownership probably attracts a different level of management talent, persons who want to see a direct relationship between their efforts and their personal income.
- This makes every unit manager a capitalist and a part owner without the risks.
- Allows persons with enterprise spirit to enjoy it with minimal investment and maximum protection from failure.

Practice Quiz

TRUE OR FALSE
On the following questions, answer whether the statement provided is true or false.

T   F   1. Experience has shown that the most practical and immediately beneficial way of training restaurant employees is the learner-controlled instruction method.

T   F   2. Most training programs involve comprehensible step-by-step job learning that utilize job checklists and differing styles of management control.

T   F   3. The Foodservice Management Professional Credential (FMP) has minimum requirements and a certification examination with five sections that must be passed before the certification is awarded.

T   F   4. Surprise quizzes and examinations are good ways to ensure performance at a high level.

T   F   5. Using part-time workers results in giving less training.

T   F   6. It should be expected that there will be periods during the training when no observable progress is made.

T   F   7.   Many believe the learner-controlled instruction method is less costly than classroom instruction and reflects employees' different levels of motivation, energy, and ability.

T   F   8.   A piece of the action is the term used by some restaurants in encouraging unit managers to acquire through purchase a percentage of the store they manage.

T   F   9.   The restaurant has an obligation to provide employees with the skills necessary to perform the job.

T   F   10.   The Bureau of Labor Statistics reports that well under half of all persons employed in foodservice occupations work part time.

FILL IN THE BLANKS: KEY TERM REVIEW

On the following questions, fill in the blank with the most appropriate key term.

1.   _____ development deals with principles and policies that managers use in relating to employees and customers.

2.   A well-planned _____ program helps new employees become acquainted with the restaurant and feel a part of it, it is important to establish a bond between the new employee and the restaurant.

3.   The objective in _____ employees is to produce desired behavior—attitudes and skills appropriate for producing food and service that pleases the restaurant's clientele.

4.   Closely related to role-playing, which has been around a long time, _____ is a technique that depicts the right way to handle personnel problems, shows how to interview and evaluate applicants, and demonstrates decision-making.

5.   The _____ model views restaurant managers as coaches, they are engaged in informal training much of the time—showing, telling, correcting, praising, and providing direction.

6.   Employee _____ promotes problem-solving ability and provides analytical skills, new perceptions, and methodologies.

7.   _____ transforms problems into challenges, excites the imagination, calls on pride, develops a sense of accomplishment and achievement, and provides opportunities to overcome obstacles.

8.   _____ provides learning material that can be studied and learned by individuals at their own pace.

MULTIPLE CHOICE QUESTIONS: CONCEPT REVIEW

On the following questions, circle the choice that best answers the question.

1. Tipping in New York City is probably higher than in most American cities, close to:
    a. 10%
    b. 15%
    c. 20%
    d. 25%

2. The term used by some restaurants in encouraging unit managers to acquire through purchase a percentage of the store they manage is:
    a. "A piece of the action."
    b. "Motivate through percentage."
    c. "Leadership with motives."
    d. "Management to ownership"..

3. Behavior modification is based on:
    a. college population studies.
    b. studies on restaurant guests.
    c. animal studies.
    d. none of the above.

4. The first goal for an orientation program is to:
    a. explain and show what is expected of employees.
    b. ensure that employees know what to do and who to ask when unsure.
    c. explain the company history, philosophy, mission, goals, and objectives.
    d. none of the above.

5. At one restaurant in Sarasota, Florida, the owner wanted to increase sales at his restaurants by $0.50 per guest. That goal was:
    a. never reached.
    b. reached after months of training.
    c. reached after the servers were told they were being watched.
    d. reached one week after the servers participated in a sales training program.

6. The Foodservice Management Professional Credential exam covers:
    a. three areas.
    b. four areas.
    c. five areas.
    d. six areas.

7. Which of the following is a true statement?
   a. In setting instructional goals, give trainees more work than they can accomplish so that they will work toward high standards.
   b. A trainer should spend as much or more time in preparation to train as in actual instruction.
   c. Popular persons are certain to make good trainers.
   d. A person who performs well on the job is qualified to teach others the skills needed for the job.

8. Closely related to role playing, which has been around a long time, which of the following is a technique that depicts the right way to handle personnel problems, shows how to interview and evaluate applicants, and demonstrates decision making?
   a. behavior modeling
   b. awareness training
   c. learner controlled instruction
   d. coaching

9. The Bureau of Labor Statistic reports that:
   a. Well over half of all persons employed in the foodservice industry work part time.
   b. In the quick service segment, the proportion of part-timers is higher.
   c. Part-time employees are good for the industry because they can be scheduled to fit into peaks and valleys of sales.
   d. All of the above

10. The Educational Foundation of the National Restaurant Association has developed informational video tapes and CD-ROMs. Topics areas include all of the following except:
    a. Alcohol awareness training.
    b. Back-of-the-house-training.
    c. Wine Training.
    d. Profits from people.

11. The word "manage" implies:
    a. purpose.
    b. mobilization of resources.
    c. punishment.
    d. a and b.

12. Which of the following is a program in which employees are given job standards to achieve and asked to reach the standards at their own pace?
    a. behavior modeling
    b. awareness training
    c. learner controlled instruction
    d. coaching

13. Which of the following is a false statement?
    a. The trainer should have written task instructions before beginning to teach and should list the key points around which instructions are built.
    b. After a task is learned, ask trainees for suggestions on how to improve the task.
    c. The best way to handle a cocky trainee is to embarrass the person in front of others.
    d. The trainer should learn what the employee already knows about the job before starting to train.

14. Employee development programs deal with:
    a. perspectives.
    b. attitudes.
    c. feelings.
    d. all the above.

15. Behavior modification theory urges:
    a. an immediate reward for whatever behavior is desired.
    b. an immediate punishment for undesirable behavior.
    c. no rewards.
    d. b and c

SHORT ANSWER QUESTIONS

1. Why is it important to have a well-planned orientation program? _____

_____

_____

_____

2. Describe the benefits and the drawbacks of hiring part-time employees. _____

_____

_____

_____

3. What is the main objective in training and development? _____

_____

_____

_____

4. Name the 3 technique used to train new employees. _____

_____

_____

_____

STUDY GUIDE ANSWER KEY

CHAPTER 1

TRUE OR FALSE
1. True
2. True
3. False
4. True
5. False

6. True
7. True
8. False
9. False
10. False

FILL IN THE BLANKS: KEY TERM REVIEW
1. flip
2. concept
3. franchise
4. quality control
5. restorantes or restoratives

MULTIPLE CHOICE QUESTIONS: CONCEPT REVIEW
1. b
2. a
3. c
4. d
5. c

6. b
7. d
8. b
9. d
10. a

11. a
12. d
13. b
14. d
15. a

SHORT ANSWER QUESTIONS
1. The term restaurant came to the United States in 1794 via a French refugee from the guillotine, Jean-Baptiste Gilbert Paypalt. Paypalt set up what must have been the first French restaurant in this country, Julien's Restaurator, in Boston.
2. *Advantages:* High: Potential rewards (psychological and financial).
   Disadvantages: High: Financial risk, stress, psychological cost of failure.
3. *Advantages:* High: Potential rewards (psychological and financial), freedom.
   Disadvantages: High: Financial risk, stress, psychological cost of failure.
4. *Advantages:* Less risk of failure since operation has been tested in market place. Potential rewards (psychological and financial).
   Disadvantages: Financial risk, stress, psychological cost of failure.
5. *Advantages:* No original investment needed; No financial risk; Some potential rewards.
   Disadvantages: Experience is needed; There is stress, some psychological costs of failure, and a smaller amount of financial reward.

CHAPTER 2

TRUE OR FALSE
1. True
2. False
3. True
4. False
5. True

6. False
7. True
8. True
9. True
10. True

FILL IN THE BLANKS: KEY TERM REVIEW
1. Bakery-cafés
2. Centralization
3. Independent restaurant
4. Quick-service restaurant
5. Ethnic restaurant
6. Steakhouse
7. Casual Restaurant
8. Theme restaurants
9. Fast Casual
10. Fine-dining
11. Chef-owned
12. Family restaurants

MULTIPLE CHOICE QUESTIONS: CONCEPT REVIEW
1. c
2. b
3. a
4. b
5. c

6. b
7. d
8. a
9. a
10. c

11. a
12. c
13. d
14. a
15. d

SHORT ANSWER QUESTIONS
1. The advantages include recognition in the marketplace; greater advertising clout; sophisticated systems development; discounted purchasing and when franchising; various kinds of assistance.
2. Defining traits are the use of high quality ingredients; fresh made to order menu items; healthful options; limited or self-serving formats; upscale décor and carryout meals. Fast casual restaurants include: Ex. Rubios Fresh Mexican Grill, Chevy's Fresh Mex, La Salsa, Texas-based Freebirds World Burrito. Panera, etc.
3. Franchising involves the least financial risk in that the restaurant format, including building design, menu, and marketing plans, already have been tested in the marketplace. Franchise restaurants are less likely to go "belly up" than independent restaurants. The reason is that the concept is proven and the operating procedures are established with all (or most) of

the kinks worked out. Training is provided, and marketing and management support are available.

4. Chefs who own restaurants have the advantage of having an experienced, highly motivated person in charge, hopefully helped by a spouse or partner equally interested in the restaurant's success. However, hundreds of chefs are less knowledgeable about costs, marketing, and "the numbers" that are requisite for a restaurant's success. Many chef-owners learn the hard way that location and other factors are just as important for success as food preparation and presentation.

5. The advantage for the independent restaurateur is that they can "do their own thing" in terms of concept development, menus, décor, and so on.

CHAPTER 3

TRUE OR FALSE

1. True
2. True
3. True
4. False
5. False

6. True
7. True
8. False
9. False
10. True

FILL IN THE BLANKS: KEY TERM REVIEW

1. Topographical survey
2. Restaurant concepts
3. Mission statement
4. Protect the restaurants name
5. Different and better.
6. sequence of restaurant development
7. Profitable
8. Degree of service

MULTIPLE CHOICE QUESTIONS: CONCEPT REVIEW

1. a
2. b
3. a
4. b
5. c

6. a
7. c
8. a
9. d
10. b

11. c
12. c
13. a
14. b
15. d

SHORT ANSWER QUESTIONS

1. Sequence of Restaurant Development
    1. Business marketing initiated
    2. Layout and equipment planned
    3. Menu determined
    4. First architectural sketches made
    5. Licensing and approvals sought
    6. Financing arranged
    7. Working blueprints developed
    8. Contracts for bidding
    9. Contractor selected
    10. Construction or remodeling begun
    11. Furnishing and equipment ordered
    12. Key personnel hired
    13. Hourly employees selected and trained
    14. Restaurant opened
2. The designer performs the following services:

- Basic floor plan
- Equipment schedule
- Electrical requirements
- Plumbing requirements
- Equipment
- Equipment elevations
- Refrigeration requirements
- Exhaust and in-take requirements

3. The most profitable restaurants are in quick-service category because they have:
    - Predominantly minimum-wage personnel
    - High sales volume
    - The use of systems
    - Excellent marketing

4. Location Criteria
    - Proper zoning.
    - Drainage, sewage, utilities.
    - Minimal size.
    - Length of lease.
    - Excessive traffic speed.
    - Access from a highway or street.
    - Visibility from both sides of the street.
    - Market population.
    - Family income.
    - Growth or decline of the area.
    - Competition from comparable restaurants.
    - The restaurant row or cluster concept.

CHAPTER 4

TRUE OR FALSE
1. True
2. True
3. False
4. False
5. False
6. True
7. False
8. False
9. True
10. True

FILL IN THE BLANKS: KEY TERM REVIEW
1. atmospherics
2. business plan
3. Strategies or action plans
4. position
5. product levels
6. Cost-based pricing
7. product life cycle
8. Marketing
9. Product positioning
10. restaurant differentiation
11. Promotion
12. market, segmented
13. prime costs
14. Product analysis
15. marketing philosophy

MULTIPLE CHOICE QUESTIONS: CONCEPT REVIEW
1. d
2. c
3. a
4. c
5. d
6. b
7. d
8. d
9. d
10. a
11. d
12. b
13. b
14. a
15. d

SHORT ANSWER QUESTIONS
1. Creating a business plan increases the probability of success; helps to gain financing; is a communication tool to and for potential investors; defines the operational purpose; establishes a mission statement; establishes goals for each operational unit; outlines strategies to achieve goals.
2. Sales focuses on the needs of the seller whereas marketing focuses on the needs of the buyer.
3. A market assessment analyzes the needs of the community, potential guests, and the competition.
4. Geographical; demographic, behavior.
5. Place, product, price, promotion.

CHAPTER 5

TRUE OR FALSE

1. False
2. True
3. False
4. False
5. False

6. True
7. False
8. True
9. True
10. True

FILL IN THE BLANKS: KEY TERM REVIEW

1. Stockpile credit
2. capitol
3. liability
4. MESBICs
5. leased
6. compensating balance
7. SCORE
8. SBICs
9. interest rates
10. collateral

MULTIPLE CHOICE QUESTIONS: CONCEPT REVIEW

1. a
2. c
3. c
4. d
5. d

6. c
7. a
8. b
9. a
10. b

11. c
12. a
13. d
14. b
15. c

SHORT ANSWER QUESTIONS

1. The two values should be considered separately. Real estate value is usually determined by competitive values in the community. A restaurant buyer is much concerned with the real estate value, a potential lessee less so. A restaurant building may actually detract from the real estate value, especially if the building has failed as a restaurant one or several times or is unattractive. The real estate value may be greater than the operational value.
2. $64,000 (8,000 × $8)
3. $768,000 ($64,000 × 12)
4. Less capital is required for leasing than for building or buying. The beginner reduces the investment and, should the venture fail, reduces loss.

CHAPTER 6

TRUE OR FALSE
1. True
2. True
3. True
4. False
5. False
6. False
7. True
8. False
9. True
10. True

FILL IN THE BLANKS: KEY TERM REVIEW
1. Employment Retirement Income Security Act (ERISA)
2. depreciation
3. fringe benefits
4. Federal Wage and Hour Law
5. Americans with Disabilities Act (ADA)
6. Age Discrimination in Employment Act
7. Partnerships
8. Civil Rights Act of 1964
9. sole proprietorship
10. IRA
11. Limited
12. Federal Equal Pay Act of 1963

MULTIPLE CHOICE QUESTIONS: CONCEPT REVIEW
1. c
2. d
3. d
4. a
5. b
6. b
7. a
8. b
9. d
10. c
11. c
12. d
13. d
14. c
15. a

SHORT ANSWER QUESTIONS
1. Workers' compensation provides income and medical benefits to accident victims or their dependents regardless of fault, provided the accident happened on the job. Employers pay an insurance premium based on the number of employees and the kind of work performed.
2. It prevents companies from arbitrarily dismissing employees engaged in union activity.
3. Age 14; the Federal Equal Pay Act of 1963
4. Bona fide meal periods, ordinarily 30 minutes, are not counted as hours worked—time that must be paid for by the employer. If, during a meal period, the employee is frequently interrupted by calls to duty, the meal period must be counted as hours worked and compensation paid.

CHAPTER 7

TRUE OR FALSE
1. True
2. False
3. False
4. False
5. True
6. True
7. True
8. False
9. True
10. True

FILL IN THE BLANKS: KEY TERM REVIEW
1. consistency
2. price
3. nutritional value
4. Vegetarian
5. available
6. Flavor
7. Raw fare
8. Accuracy in the menu
9. degustation
10. contribution margin
11. capability
12. Menu design and layout
13. Vegan
14. food cost percentage
15. equipment

MULTIPLE CHOICE QUESTIONS: CONCEPT REVIEW
1. d
2. d
3. a
4. d
5. c
6. c
7. c
8. b
9. d
10. a
11. b
12. d
13. b
14. c
15. d

SHORT ANSWER QUESTIONS
1. A list of ingredients followed by step-by-step methods to produce a quality product.
2. Factors include amount of product; quality of product; reliability or consistency of product; uniqueness of product; product options/choices; service convenience; comfort level; reliability/consistency of service; tie-in offers and freebies.
3. The contribution margin is the difference between the sales and the cost of the item.
4. The different types of menus are dinner-house; a la carte; table d'hôte; du jour; cyclical; menus cycled every few days; California, tourist, degustation.

CHAPTER 8

TRUE OR FALSE

1. False
2. True
3. True
4. True
5. False

6. False
7. False
8. True
9. False
10. True

FILL IN THE BLANKS: KEY TERM REVIEW

1. refrigerator or freezer
2. cook-chill
3. conveyor broiler
4. Slow cooking
5. Low-temperature ovens
6. traditional range
7. categories of kitchen equipment
8. Sous vide
9. deep fryers
10. forced-air convection oven

MULTIPLE CHOICE QUESTIONS: CONCEPT REVIEW

1. d
2. c
3. b
4. b
5. a

6. d
7. b
8. a
9. b
10. d

11. a
12. d
13. c
14. c
15. d

SHORT ANSWER QUESTIONS

1. To minimize the number of steps taken by kitchen personnel and wait staff.
2. Receiving and storing food; fabricating and preparing food; preparing and processing food; assembling, holding and serving food; cleaning up the kitchen and kitchenware.
3. It is important to assure the public that eating in restaurants is safe.

CHAPTER 9

TRUE OR FALSE
1. False
2. True
3. True
4. False
5. True
6. True
7. False
8. False
9. True
10. True

FILL IN THE BLANKS: KEY TERM REVIEW
1. Par stock
2. Food purchasing system
3. Food specification/ standards
4. Combination
5. Purchasing
6. No. 1.
7. Fancy
8. No. 3.
9. Reorder point
10. Inventory

MULTIPLE CHOICE QUESTIONS: CONCEPT REVIEW
1. b
2. b
3. c
4. b
5. c
6. d
7. a
8. a
9. d
10. d
11. d
12. a
13. a
14. a
15. c

SHORT ANSWER QUESTIONS
1. Steps in a Food Purchasing System
   - Determine the quality of food standards required to serve the market.
   - Develop product specifications.
   - Gather product-availability information.
   - Have alternate suppliers in mind.
   - Select a person to order and receive supplies.
2. Steps in a Purchasing System
   - Set up storage space for maximum utilization.
   - Establish the amount needed to be stocked- par stock – each item.
   - Set up inventory system.
   - Decide on optimal delivery size to reduce cost of delivery and handling.
   - Check all inventories for quality and quantity/weight.
   - Tie inventory control and cost control system together.

3. Full-line purveyors carry a large line of supplies; offer more one stop shopping; save time; allow for simplified billing
4. Co-op Buying
   – Supplies products at cost, plus enough of a markup to cover the cooperative's cost.
   – Nonprofit
   – Lower cost than profit
5. Buying by Specification
   • Each operation needs a quality of food that fits its market.
   • The quality needed varies with the market and also with the food item being produced.
     – Canned vegetables used in a made-up dish need not be of fancy grade.
     – Meat for grinding into hamburger may well come from U.S. good or even lower-graded meat and still be satisfactory.

CHAPTER 10

TRUE OR FALSE
1. False
2. True
3. False
4. True
5. True

6. False
7. True
8. True
9. False
10. True

FILL IN THE BLANKS: KEY TERM REVIEW
1. haute cuisine
2. Production
3. pathogens
4. fusion cuisine
5. cooking line
6. mise-en-place
7. prep sheets or production sheets
8. par levels
9. French
10. the last-in, first-out (LIFO), first-in, first-out (FIFO)

MULTIPLE CHOICE QUESTIONS: CONCEPT REVIEW
1. b
2. b
3. b
4. b
5. c

6. c
7. d
8. a
9. a
10. d

11. a
12. b
13. d
14. a
15. d

SHORT ANSWER QUESTIONS
1. Mise en place means the assembly of ingredients and equipment for the recipe. Production starts here because the backbone for every service in the restaurant is the ingredients being 'prepped' for all the recipes.
2. Time/temperature abuse; cross-contamination; poor personal hygiene.
3. Restaurant chemicals like detergents and sanitizers.
   Preservatives and additives.
   Acidic reaction of foods with metal-lined containers.
   Contamination of food with toxic metals.
4. Viruses do not require a hazardous food in order to survive.
   - They can survive on any food or surface, do not multiply, and are not as affected by heat or cold, as are bacteria.
   - They simply use the food or other surface as means of transportation.
   - Once the virus enters a body cell, it takes over, forcing the cell to assist in the production of more viruses.

CHAPTER 11

TRUE OR FALSE
1. True
2. True
3. True
4. False
5. True
6. False
7. False
8. True
9. False
10. True

FILL IN THE BLANKS: KEY TERM REVIEW
1. Service encounter
2. Difficult Guest
3. Social distance
4. Eye contact
5. Team
6. soft sell
7. Tact

MULTIPLE CHOICE QUESTIONS: CONCEPT REVIEW
1. d
2. c
3. a
4. b
5. b
6. c
7. a
8. c
9. a
10. d
11. b
12. b
13. c
14. d
15. b

SHORT ANSWER QUESTIONS
1. What Makes a Good Server
   - Personality.
   - Team orientation.
   - Technical knowledge of product/tableside confidence.
   - Knowledge of how to read guests and anticipate their needs.
   - Knowledge of the finer points of service.
2. The approach is, "What can I do to help?"
3.
   1. Tell the truth.
   2. Bend the rules.
   3. Listen actively.
   4. Put pen to paper.
   5. Master the moments of truth.
   6. Be a fantastic fixer.
   7. Never underestimate the value of a thank you.
4. The main part of the host/hostess's job is to represent the restaurant by offering a friendly greeting and facilitating the seating of guests.
5. Strategies for Handling Complaints
   - Remain calm.
   - Listen.
   - Empathize.
   - Control your voice.
   - Get the facts.
   - Take care of the problem immediately.
   - If you take back an entrée, offer to keep the meals of the other diners warm in the kitchen, so that the group can eat together.

CHAPTER 12

TRUE OR FALSE
1. True
2. True
3. False
4. False
5. False
6. True
7. False
8. False
9. True
10. False

FILL IN THE BLANKS: KEY TERM REVIEW
1. responsible alcoholic beverage service
2. front bar, back bar, under bar
3. Wine
4. speed gun
5. well (or pouring)
6. fining
7. fortified wines
8. clarified
9. pull handle
10. back bar

MULTIPLE CHOICE QUESTIONS: CONCEPT REVIEW
1. a
2. d
3. b
4. d
5. b
6. c
7. c
8. a
9. d
10. c
11. d
12. b
13. a
14. d
15. a

SHORT ANSWER QUESTIONS
1. Wine is made in six steps: Crushing, fermenting, racking, maturing, filtering, and bottling.
2. 1. Crushing: Grapes are crushed and the juice is extracted.
   2. Fermenting: A natural thing caused by yeasts on the skins of the grapes. The yeast converts the sugar in the grapes to ethyl alcohol, until little or no sugar is left in the wine.
   3. Racking: The wine is put into racks and settles before being poured into stainless steel vats or oak barrels.
   4. Maturing: The wine is put into stainless steel vat or oak barrels to age.
   5. Filtering: The wine is stabilized and solids are removed.
   6. Bottling: The wine is put into its bottle!
3. Fine vintage wines are kept for a few years to further mature in the bottle and drunk at their peak—several years later.
4. • Welcoming the guest, taking and preparing the drink and food orders in a friendly manner.
   • Making sure that the drink is rung up and paid for.

- Keeping the bar and bar area clean, including glassware.
- Prepping enough fruit, juices, liquor and other stock for the shift.
- Replacing any used stock for the next shift.
- Cutting off or refusing to serve anyone who appears intoxicated, then making arrangements for the person to get home safely.
- Providing the guests with entertaining conversation.
- Making drinks for the servers and providing them with change.
- Taking inventory of all beer and liquor bottles at the end of shift.
- Remembering everyone's name!

5. The bartender is responsible for cutting off or refusing to serve anyone who appears intoxicated. Then should make arrangements for the person to get home safely and prevent the person from driving. Another good practice is to encourage food consumption. Finally, all incidents of concern should be recorded.

CHAPTER 13

TRUE OR FALSE
1. True
2. True
3. True
4. False
5. True

6. False
7. True
8. True
9. False
10. True

FILL IN THE BLANKS: KEY TERM REVIEW
1. Back of the house
2. PDA (personal digital assistant)
3. Labor management systems
4. POS (point-of-sale)
5. menu management
6. E-learning

MULTIPLE CHOICE QUESTIONS: CONCEPT REVIEW
1. a
2. c
3. a
4. a
5. c

6. b
7. b
8. c
9. b
10. a

11. c
12. d
13. a
14. d
15. d

SHORT ANSWER QUESTIONS
1. Once the manager completes the schedule, associates cannot clock in more than ten minutes early or five minutes late without a manager's override. This prevents people from coming in early and taking a socializing break out back.

2. Labor management systems include a module to monitor applications (which can now be online and paperless), recruitment, personnel information, I-9 status, tax status, availability, vacation, and benefit information. Labor management systems also do the scheduling based on the forecasted volume of business.

3. They use MenuLink to evaluate managers' produce purchasing, test proposed recipe and pricing changes, and compare actual to expected food usage.

4. When one store needs to borrow material from another store, a transfer is generated. The new feature provides a method in which the receiving store can process the transfer in the same general way as if the materials were purchased from a food vendor who is enabled for electronic ordering and invoicing.

CHAPTER 14

TRUE OR FALSE
1. True
2. True
3. False
4. True
5. False

6. True
7. False
8. True
9. False
10. True

FILL IN THE BLANKS: KEY TERM REVIEW
1. Controllable expenses
2. labor cost
3. pass
4. production sheet
5. liquor control
6. back of the house
7. key result area (KSA)
8. beverage cost percentage
9. Front of the house
10. guest count

MULTIPLE CHOICE QUESTIONS: CONCEPT REVIEW
1. d
2. b
3. a
4. d
5. a

6. d
7. b
8. a
9. c
10. c

11. b
12. b
13. a
14. a
15. c

SHORT ANSWER QUESTIONS
1. The term used to describe the various expenses that can be changed in the short term.
2. They include Variable costs; Payroll; Operating expenses; Marketing; Heat; Light; Repairs; Maintenance
3. The formula for doing the food cost percentage is Cost $\div$ Sales $\times$ 100.
4. Payroll and related costs fall into two categories:
   - Variable (percentage ratio to payroll).
   - Fixed (dollar amount per employee on the payroll).

CHAPTER 15

TRUE OR FALSE

1. True
2. False
3. True
4. False
5. True
6. False
7. False
8. False
9. True
10. True

FILL IN THE BLANKS: KEY TERM REVIEW

1. Americans with Disabilities Act (ADA)
2. Selection
3. job specification
4. Recruitment
5. task
6. task and job analysis
7. Job specifications
8. job
9. Interviewing
10. Civil rights laws

MULTIPLE CHOICE QUESTIONS: CONCEPT REVIEW

1. c
2. c
3. d
4. c
5. c
6. b
7. d
8. c
9. c
10. c
11. a
12. d
13. b
14. b
15. a

SHORT ANSWER QUESTIONS

1. Three Main Hiring Objectives
   - Hire people who project an image and attitude appropriate for your restaurant.
   - Hire people who will work with you rather than spend their time fighting your rules, procedures, and system.
   - Hire people whose personal and financial requirements are a good fit with the hours and positions you are hiring for.
2. It lists the education and technical/conceptual skills a person needs to satisfactorily perform the requirements of the job. Once the tasks performed in a job are described, a separate section of the job description form can be developed.
3. A job interview should give the employer enough information to determine of the applicant is capable of doing the job.
4. Determining the eligibility and suitability of a perspective employee (how well they will do the job and how well they will fit in with the team).

CHAPTER 16

TRUE OR FALSE
1. False
2. True
3. True
4. False
5. False
6. True
7. True
8. True
9. True
10. False

FILL IN THE BLANKS: KEY TERM REVIEW
1. Management
2. orientation
3. training and developing
4. behavior modeling
5. manager as coach
6. development
7. Leadership
8. Learner-controlled instruction

MULTIPLE CHOICE QUESTIONS: CONCEPT REVIEW
1. c
2. a
3. c
4. c
5. d
6. c
7. b
8. a
9. d
10. d
11. d
12. c
13. c
14. d
15. a

SHORT ANSWER QUESTIONS
1. A well-planned orientation program helps new employees become acquainted with the restaurant and feel a part of it.
2. Varying opinions but may include:
   - Benefits include: not having to pay benefits, they can be scheduled to fit the peaks and valleys in sales.
   - Drawbacks include: possible lack of continuity, increases the need for training.
3. The objective in training and developing employees is to produce desired behavior—attitudes and skills appropriate for producing food and service that pleases the restaurant's clientele. Much learning can be programmed; employees are trained to follow a sequence of behavior.
4. Behavior modeling; learner-controlled instruction; and coaching.